Information Architecture

A Multidisciplinary Text Book

INFORMATION ARCHITECTURE

A Multidisciplinary Text Book

By

Saravanan T.

Assistant Professor,
Department of Library & Information Science,
Annamalai University,
Annamalai Nagar
Chidambaram,
Tamilnadu-608002

Ess Ess Publications
New Delhi

Information Architecture
A Multidisciplinary Textbook

ISBN: 978-81-7000-664-0

Rs.595/-

First Published 2012

Published by:
Ess Ess Publications
4831/24, Ansari Road,
Darya Ganj,
New Delhi-110 002.
INDIA
Phones: 23260807, 41563444
Fax: 41563334
E-mail: info@essessreference.com
www.essessreference.com

Cover Design by *Patch Creative Unit*

Printed and bound in India at Salasar Imaging Systems.

This book is dedicated to

DR. M. G. RAMACHANDRAN(LATE)

Tamil Film- Ever Green Hero

&

Former Chief Minister

Tamilnadu-India

ANNAMALAI UNIVERSITY

Dr.M.RATHINASABAPATHI,M.Sc,(Engg.),Ph.D.,M.I.E,
REGISTRAR

ANNAMALAINAGAR-608 002 INDIA
Ph: off: 04144-238259 Fax:04144-238080

Foreword

Dr.T.Saravanan is a prolific writer. His latest book is this one: "Information Architecture: For Successful Conferences/Seminars - - A Multidisciplinary Text Book." Generally, his books showcase the impact of Information Technology on various aspects of knowledge. IT which has revolutionized the acquisition and dissemination of knowledge is found to be immensely useful in Library and Information Science. With a keen observation and research acumen, he describes and demonstrates in this book, how WinISIS concepts and application can be used to conduct successfully seminars and conferences. The package approved and developed by UNESCO has been harnessed to serve for the Indian situation, volatile and unpredictable. Also he illustrates how exigencies can be met on adopting WinISIS package. I hope that the knowledge of this book will enable the organizers of conferences and seminars to conduct them successfully and smoothly. I am sure that this book will soon turn into a rule –book for the organizers, across the borders of various disciplines.

Station: Annamalainagar

Date : 18-Nov-2010

Dr.M.Rathinasabapathi

Contents

List of Tables

List of Screen Shots

Preface

Information architecture is a complex process and it requires an effective organization to succeed. Here skills play a vital role to manage the complexity. In the modern era, technology offers more ways through which the suitable one could be carefully picked to face the complexity, whereas in the traditional one the professionals would not have had these features to build the information architecture to accomplish these tasks. The ways which are adopted by me to organize information for the seminar may provide you the maximum ideas about an event. This approach has been designed to offer maximum flexibility. I trust that this work will offer many advantages to the readers of this book, since it concentrates on the following areas:

1. Emphasis on identification of the database tool and organizing the data
2. With 206 records, related items are explored to capture the practical concepts and implementation.
3. The optimal utilization of system and software permits for larger and more realistic designs and decision making.

Many readers will not be able to understand the general context in the application package. Especially the application package 'WinISIS®' which has been adopted by me in this book would be little bit tough to them, as it requires a prior knowledge in it. In chapter 3 the subsection Pascal program requires high level programming knowledge to carry out the procedures which have been discussed in it. However, designers could carry out the same things to maintain their data as discussed in this book with the help of some other database tools in which they feel that they are familiar or they have prior experience.

An essential aspect of my approach is teaching students the concepts of WinISIS® application package which was developed by UNESCO. While teaching the WinISIS® package to my students, I would always refer the term as "WinISIS® is like a blank white notebook where you could build your dreams whatever they may be".

As you know that any blank white paper allows us to write anything as per our requirements such as Numeric, Texts, images etc., could be done on it. It means there is no restriction to structure our ideas. The WinISIS® application package permits us to make our choices. However the selection of the database is purely optional. But you could capture some guidelines from the ways which I have got from my own experience that has been briefly discussed in detail.

This book is believed to make anyone an achiever, who wants to make his/her conferences/seminars simple, compact, and successful. I got this idea when I structured a database for the UGC-Sponsored national level seminar program, organized by our discipline by using WinISIS®-UNESCO developed Application Package. That's when I realized the necessity of having this kind of book, which enables people who are keen to take up conferences/seminars in a successful track, whatever the discipline they may belong to. This book covers many concepts that are essential to structure the database as maximum in depth and provides details in both the theoretical and practical aspects.

The book contains six chapters:

Chapter 1: Introduction: This chapter gives some fundamentals on Information needs, past and present scenarios. The general database concepts and an outline of WinISIS® Application package are also included.

Chapter 2: Information Architecture: Database Structure-This chapter focuses on the various stages to be structured to accomplish the task.

Chapter 3: Data Organization: This chapter discusses the steps as to how a database designer could architect the data which are related to the Conferences /Seminar by using WinISIS® Application package or any other application in the right track. The practical experiences have become samples here with enough screen shots.

Chapter 4: Reports Organization: This chapter explores varieties of outputs which have been generated for the event with the WinISIS® application package.

Chapter 5: Problems Identified: This chapter brings some of the problems which have been faced by the organizers/designers while organizing data using the database. Further this part also provides suitable solutions for the observed different kinds of problems, which may enable one to be aware of them as well as to show more attention in their assignments.

Chapter 6: Recap: This chapter summarizes the major routines which are concerned with the Information architecture.

Conclusion: In this part an overview of all the issues opted in this book are offered.

As a practical guideline there is a need for the screenshots to understand the concepts which have also been discussed in this book. Keeping these things in the mind enough screenshots have been formulated, wherever they are required for better capturing of the concepts which are concerned with information architecture.

LEARNING RESOURCES

1. CDS/ISIS for Windows Reference manual (version 1.3), *Paris, UNESCO, 1998.*
2. WinISIS - Supplement to the Reference Manual: versions 1.0-1.3. *Paris, UNESCO, November 1998*
3. *Andrew Buxton and Alan Hopkinson*, The CDS/ISIS for Windows Handbook, *Paris, UNESCO*, September 2001.
4. *Nowicki, Zbigniew M*. New Features of the WinISIS System: Guidebook for Users of CDS/ISIS for DOS, *Geneva, International Trade Centre, 2001.*
5. WinISIS® 1.5® (Build num. 3) Changes and News since Winisis 1.311, Paris, UNESCO, 23 December 2003.
6. CDS/ISIS for Windows Reference Manual(Build num.3- versions 1.5), Revised by Ben Winnubst, New Zealand, June 2004.

WinISIS® is the registered trademark of UNESCO.

Microsoft Word®, Microsoft Excel®, Microsoft Access®, and Windows® are registered trademarks of Microsoft Corporation.

Acknowledgments

Though I painfully worked my way up from the beginning of this book, there have been a great many kind souls who were behind my contribution. The roles of my parents, wife Vasuki Devi, S and son Saran, R.T.S while this book was being structured during the past one year were unforgettable. Let me acknowledge the act of all of them with particular emphasis on the following.

The authorities of Annamalai University, Tamilnadu, India, where I have been in service as a faculty member since 2002, and who kindly considered, accepted my request and granted permission along with the foreword to bring out this edition.

Editors, Ess Ess Publications, who are behind the scenes and without their kind support this book, would not have seen the day.

Professor Emeritus Subramanian, Department of Library and Information Science, Madurai Kamaraj University, Tamilnadu, India, who encouraged me to carry out the LIS Course.

Professor Emeritus Srimurugan A, Department of Library and Information Science, Madurai Kamaraj University, Tamilnadu, India, who is behind my subject development. I have learnt many things from him when I was doing LIS Course.

Professor Emeritus Dr. Kamalakara Rao A. P., Former Principal, TNC Arts & Science college in Chennai, Tamilnadu, India, who ignited my career as a Founder Librarian.

Dr. Nagarajan M, Professor & Head, Department of Library and Information Science, Annamalai University, Tamilnadu, India, who is always encouraging me to carry out this kind of academic activities.

Professor Dr. Anbanandam M, Department of English, Annamalai University, Tamilnadu ,India, who is always interested in my career development.

Mr. Senthilkumar, V and Mr. Sankaranarayanan D, Assistant Professors, Dept. of Library and Information Science, who offered their kind support in all the times.

The author extends his thanks to the following people who are always interested with his successful development and worked with him since he has been working as a Founder Librarian in TN College of Arts and Science, Chennai, Tamilnadu, India.

Mrs.Mallika Ilangovan, Former Faculty member in English; Mrs. Umamaheswari , Head & Mrs. Uma Arivazhagan, Former Faculty member in Tamil; Mrs. Shalinidevi , Head & Mrs. Jeyasudha, Faculty member in Corporate Secretary ship; Mr. Arockiaraj, Former Head, Department of Computer science;

The author thanks to his friends who are with him since the beginning of his school & higher education in the state of Tamilnadu.

Mr.Azhagumurugan A and Mr.Surulivel-Kodaikannal; Mr.Velrajan R(Cinematographer (SICA)) *- Chennai; Mr. Kamatchi V and Mr.Masanam M-Elumalai; Mr.Soundarajan M-Karur; Mr.Ganesan S, Mr.Akbar A and Mr.Ramakrishnan-*

Kombai; Mr.Rajkumar-Madurai; Mr. Senthil D-Paramakudi; Mr.Thirupathiraj-Rajapalayam; Mr. Shanmugaraj-Chennai.

I always like to follow up the inspirational words which have been given by the experts whoever they maybe to reach my target when I have an idea to take up any kind of tasks and these terms enabled me to carry out my works in an easier, compact way and also reduced my burdens, removed the interruptions which were faced by me while moving on the track with work load. The following expressions would always be in my mind:

Arise, awake and stop not till the goal is reached.

All power is within you; you can do anything and everything.

Believe in that, do not believe that you are weak.

Stand up and express the divinity within you.

— Swami Vivekananda

"Unnai Arinthal Nee Unnai Arinthal" (if you know yourself, you can fight the world)

— Dr.M.G.Ramachandran (Late) Former Chief Minister of Tamilnadu State, India.

"Welcome the criticizing comments and do not bother about them"

— Steven Spielberg, United States filmmaker. (Ref. Deccan Chronicle, South India Edition, December 2009)

"Talk less Work more" — Great Men

Finally I thank the almighty who is always behind my endeavour and comes along with me always not only while structuring this book but in every walk of my life.

Sarvanan T.

1

Introduction

The word 'growth' is perhaps controllable in many of the sectors but it is not possible for something in the world none other than 'Information'. When we imagine the growth of information whatever be the field it is concerned with, it is unbelievable nowadays. Information generators who are playing a vital role behind the growth of information are the major resources as the modern users' expectations are high rather than the early periods, and their expectations also have no boundaries. Hence the authors are not in the position to meet the users' requirements. Capturing required information has been a cumbersome process once. The traditional period clearly explores the problems, which were faced by the information seekers in those days. What do we have in our desk nowadays were not available in early days due to the lack of technology. We have to owe our thanks to technology, as we all enjoy the latest. In my own experience, I was not able to capture the required data that was related to my Ph.D research work within the stipulated period due to the non-availability of the aforesaid features.

Everyone in the world needs information. We never see a person who doesn't need information. Even a baby needs something that could be conveyed through its body language.

Nicholas and Rowlands developed a model to show the progressive stages of knowledge from data. The 4 stages are:

1. Data;
2. Information;
3. Knowledge;
4. Wisdom.

Menne-Haritz_identifies 4 sources of knowledge as consisting of:

1. Scientifically or theoretically presented knowledge potentials;
2. Practically prepared knowledge potentials;
3. Raw material for the creation of knowledge potentials;
4. Experience and Observations.

Stephen M. Mutula and Justus m. Wamukoya states that Information management is an interdisciplinary concept combining skills and resources from librarianship and information science, information technology, records management, archives and general management. It refers to the means by which an organization efficiently plans, collects, organizes, uses, controls, disseminates and disposes of its information, and the way in which it ensures that the value of that information is identified and exploited to the fullest extent. Further they say that local content has a lot of value, namely that it:

1. Serves as a means of satisfying internal needs;
2. Enhances self-reliance;
3. Helps bridge the digital divide between the information rich and information poor;
4. Enhances community access to content;

5. Has been applied in such areas as agriculture, medicine, art, technology, governance system and architectural design;
6. Mirrors real-life situation and operations;
7. Draws on local resources and makes people less dependent on outside supplies, which may be costly, scarce and irregularly available;
8. Promotes social justice so that every man or woman, no matter their race, age, background, religion, ability or disability, may have the same opportunities;
9. Provides a basis for access and participation by all in the information society;

According to Trippe and Walter content management is a tool for supporting the internal work flow process that results in publishing a website or application.

Simens states that content management as the management of content including, but not limited to digital items such as text, audio, video, graphics and links to physical resources, which allows for contribution from varied sources with points of control to ensure quality.

Wikipedia defines content management as a set of processes and technologies that support the evolutionary lifecycle of information, usually known as content.

Software Perfect identifies the following roles of content management in organizations.

1. Organizing information;
2. Knowing what Information is owned;
3. Finding that information;
4. Maintaining (current and relevant) information;

White sees knowledge management as a process of

creating, storing, sharing and reusing organizational knowledge or know-how to enable an organization to achieve its goals and objectives.

According to O'Brien "data can be defined as facts, events or transactions that have been recorded. Data can also be regarded as a raw material that has no meaning unless it is converted into information by analysis, interpretation and being put into context. Once refined, data can be regarded as information. *Knowledge Management Glossary* defines that Information can in turn be defined as data organized within a context and translated into a form with structure and meaning.

According to Wig information refers to facts and data organized to characterize a particular situation. Nonaka and Takeuchi state that information as a flow of message.

According to A.R.Pollis "Information can be effectively managed when we have a different think about it. He also pointed aout about the new phrase "IRM" ie: Information Resource Management. This term is self explanatory it denotes managing information as a resource in the same manner that other corporate resources are being managed. To do this successfully the following elements are noted by him.

1. The technology to acquire, organize and distribute information.
2. The policy of corporate body or organization concerning the use of information.
3. The framework or structure to achieve the information needs.

Further, he has pointed out the importance of decision making techniques that should assist one in tough situations. They have been categorized as six, which helps to solve management decision problems.

1. Analyze the situation: State the reason that is forcing you to make the decision

2. Design backwards: Determine what you expect the system or hardware to do.

3. Define the results: What will be the scenario if the decision works?

4. Develop your options: Look for as many different methods of achieving these results as you can; Workable or not. Should you buy a software package, use an outside service, or buy a microprocessor?

5. List your options with two columns: Advantages and Disadvantages.

6. Implement the decision: Do it!

7. Compare and evaluate: The results that you achieved with the results that you anticipated in step 2.

According to Orna, Information is what human beings transform their knowledge into when they want to communicate it to other people. It is knowledge made visible or audible in written or printed words or in speech.

Some of the words given by the Information Architecture Institute are

a. The structural design of shared information environments,

b. The art and science of organizing and labelling websites, intranets, online communities and software to support usability and find ability,

c. An emerging community of practice focused on bringing principles of design and architecture to the digital landscape.

As human beings our regular routines have been

connected to information which revolves around us always in various formats. Information architecture is typically formulated through consideration of user intention (primary tasks), and managing the relationship between the user and content or services (how tasks can be completed). A humanist perspective would place emphasis on catering solely to the user's needs however, for commercial organisations; business needs are an additional consideration. Set of rules determine what, and how and where, information will be collected, stored, processed, transmitted, presented, and used. Just imagine the world without media, newspapers, Internet or even radio communication for just an hour. What will happen? What kind of feelings have you got now? We would feel that an invisible door might be shut in front of our eyes. Our hands may be tied with some not viewable things that couldn't be expressed in words when we are not in a position to receive the information whatever it may be.

Rosenfeld L and Morville P have defined the architectural design of an information space to facilitate task completion and intuitive access to content. I have seen some persons who have expressed that they never used the library for their examination purposes. Instead they have acquired information from someone else. What does it show?. They mayn't depend on the library resources, but they need information at any cost. This attitude shows their ignorance of the library resources and also how much they are aware of it. I wonder about that what they mean by the words 'never used the library'. They suppose to need information, but not from the library. The thing is that under any circumstances they depend on the information even though they do not prefer the library. I don't mind their opinion as everyone has his/her own rights to capture information from anywhere that may or may not be a library or someone else. The purposes for which I express these items are to explore the necessity of information and the method of information gathering process that usually differs from person to person.

The invention of Internet and the Websites technology take us throughout the world without boundaries to meet our requirements. Technology is the solution to control information in an organized way, particularly, the databases that play the major role to keep any kind of data under foolproof maintenance. It is not an easy job to keep everything in our minds as we don't have supernatural powers. For instance, we can recall the names of some of our friends or relatives and their addresses as and when required. But it is not possible for one to recall their phone numbers, postal codes, important ID, etc. When the data exceed beyond the limits, there is the need for a tool like database, software etc., so as information organization and dissemination are possible.

LIS is perhaps one of the major disciplines which controls all other disciplines whatever they maybe. The information which belongs to other disciplines could be organized effectively by none other than the LIS professionals as they are familiar with indexing, classification and cataloguing concepts. A LIS professional can handle any data of any kind of discipline. Here the LIS professional is supposed not to be an expert in other discipline but he/she could organize others' data in a proper way so that the information could be utilized by someone else. With the invention of the new technological tools the burdens could be reduced from the LIS professionals and at the same time their responsibilities to organize these things in electronic form are increased. The modern users expect the LIS professionals to have adequate potential to organize the data as they don't want to get any dissatisfaction while looking for the required data.

I know that my profession belongs to Library and

Information Science and not to IT sector. But we have to travel in both tracks as they are like the two sides of a coin. Which side of the coin is essential? Can you answer this question? Of course, this may be a million dollar of question. In the modern scenario, both tracks are essential for any professionals of any discipline so as to make their target easier. I know that I am neither a full time programmer nor a database designer as my profession is different. Having fundamental knowledge of the database is a must before carrying out any task in it. Unless we are thorough in these areas it may lead the designer in the wrong track. Having adequate qualification and experience, I am always interested to work in the database by which I organize the data for the UGC sponsored seminar program conducted by our department in our premises.

I have gathered many a piece of information, while I was working with the database in the seminar program and wanted to share them with others in order to express them in a book of this kind as many of them may have the interest to run their program effectively and successfully. Some of the areas which I have discussed in this book may or may not be suitable to you as your editorial board may have different opinions and decisions that might differ from location to location. For instance, restrictions on the number of authors per paper. The board of editors have the rights to decide the said things. But the fundamentals to structure the database are common to all. The way in which I have opted to organize the data could be possible with other databases also, namely, SQL®, Oracle®, MsAccess®, etc. that depend on one's experience and preference for it. Make your choice and be sure before you start the task. I have opted WinISIS® application package, which was developed by UNESCO.

1.1. DATABASE

Plenty of definitions could be viewed about database as we live in the internet era. However, I have chosen a definition for the purpose of refreshing our knowledge of it. "A database management system is a collection of interrelated data and set of programs to access these data".

According to Michael Abbey and Michael J, Corey "A database is a collection of data files and the software that manipulates.

1.2. CDS/ISIS FOR WINDOWS

WinISIS® is a Windows version of the CDS/ISIS system that was originated by ILO in the 1960's and since 1970's it is maintained and distributed by UNESCO. In 1985 the first microcomputer version of ISIS was launched and since then it was utilized by many institutions in different countries throughout the world. The first windows based version was released in May 1995 for its experimentation and the official release of 1.31 version was launched during November 1998. Version 1.4 was circulated on CD-ROM to distributors in March 2001 and it was dated January 2001. In the year 2003, the version 1.5 (build 3) was launched.

WinISIS® version 1.5 contains the following new options and features:

1. New data entry control tools:
    a. begin and end edition coding
    b. pick list management
2. New format commands
3. In-format JPG and BMP display capabilities
4. More ISO 2709 import/export options
5. XML ready: export to XML facility

6. Dictionary prefix management and dump function
7. Faster print
8. Easier access to multimedia content (web, e-mail etc)
9. Logfiles (via the syspar.par)
10. Access to HTML help files (files not provided)

For further details please visit the UNESCO's authorized website given below:

http://www.unesco.org/isis

I am always interested to work with WinISIS® - Application package which has been developed by UNESCO for the purpose of information organization and dissemination as it has wonderful features that we may or may not get from other packages that may be a probable reason behind me for the adoption of this package. Though the application is an easy one, which requires a little bit of fundamental knowledge and experience so as we can carry out our works in it. In simple words WinISIS ® is like a new blank note book in which you can draw anything as per your requirements. You have an option to design your own database whereas the other packages may or may not have one of these features. WinISIS ® lets you to make your own choice.

Though reading and writing skills in any language can help us to go anywhere throughout the world but not into the IT tracks that leads to the wrong data manipulation and result in poor data management. I have acquired enough experiences when I have had an opportunity to develop some packages for educational purposes. Hence WinISIS® UNESCO developed package has been adopted by me to build a strong database named *SEM.Mst* on which the further processes of seminar are structured properly. This has been discussed briefly in the following chapters.

2

Information Architecture: Database Structure

Abraham Silberschatz (et al) pointed out that a primary goal of a database system is to retrieve information from and store new information in the database. Generally e-records include databases, word-processed documents, spreadsheets and e-mail. According to Stephen_M. Mutula and Justus M. Wamukoya the record management is the field of management responsible for the efficient and systematic control of the creation, receipt, maintenance, use and disposition of records, including processes for capturing and maintaining evidence of information about business activities and transactions in the form of records. IRMT defines that the e-record concept refers to recorded information, documents or data that provide evidence of policies, transactions and activities carried out in e-government and e-commerce environments. According to Roper and Millar an e-record is perceived as a digital record that can be manipulated, transmitted or processed by a computer, while the term e-records management is used to describe policies and procedures for the systematic management of records in electronic format. Cain and Millar noted that computer generated records are qualitatively different from traditional paper records. They are more vulnerable to manipulation, are harder to authenticate and their legal status can be difficult to determine compared with paper-based records.

According to ICA the electronic records lifecycle is substantially determined by choices and decisions made at the stage when the need for keeping records is identified and recordkeeping systems are designed and developed-certainly before any records are created. The UN identified the management stages in the lifecycle of e-records as follows:

Creation : Capture, storage, identification, clearance, control, security and authentication.

Communications: Communications of record internally and externally of organization.

Search and retrieval: Search, retrieval, migration, conversion, portability and control.

Preservation, maintenance and control: Maintenance and application of appraisal criteria and authorisation.

Appraisal and disposal: Appraisal, user notification and disposal of records.

With the increase in the use of computers in India, electronic documents are increasingly being recognized as evidentiary records. Consequently it is essential that the authenticity and reliability of electronic documents be preserved.

Cox notes that the management of electronic records in the developed world, especially in North America and Europe, only started gaining serious attention and recognition around the 1980s. When countries were increasingly generating e-records and using computers to manage them.

According to Reed_Australia has a thriving local automation software industry for records management. In USA (NARA) National Archives and Records Administration took the initiatives to maintain the electronic records.

In Malaysia an initiative was launched in 1999 and a human resource management information system was developed to facilitate recruitment, development, transfer, disciplinary matters, promotion and retirement.

Singapore has been able to use IT effectively to streamline business processes and improve service delivery.

According to Mnjama and Wamukoya records are valuable assets that need to be managed and protected. Besides providing essential evidence of organizational activities, transactions and decisions, records also support business functions and are critical for the assessment of organizational performance. Sound management of both paper and e-records is important in order to avoid informational gaps in public archives.

2.1. CREATING A DATABASE

As already discussed in the previous chapter, the database named '*Sem.Mst*' has been created to organize the data to carry out the seminar tasks.

According to Lancaster and Climenson, there are seven criteria to measure the performance of system design. They are:

1. Coverage (the proportion of the total useful literature on a particular topic that has been collected and indexed into the system)
2. Usability (the value of the literature included on a particular topic, in terms of such things as age, reliability and comprehensibility)

3. Recall (the ability of the system to retrieve wanted documents)
4. Precision (the ability of the system to screen out unwanted documents)
5. Response Time (the average time required to obtain a satisfactory response from the system)
6. Presentation (the form in which search results are presented)
7. User Effort (the amount of effort the user must personally expend in order to consult the system.

The relational concept has been opted by me to organize the data as it is an advanced feature that could be seen in other databases also. The purpose of the relational concept is to maintain uniformity, accuracy of the data and also it keeps us in the right track by the way of avoiding duplication of data when we have an opportunity to feed the same data in various records. Further the repeated entries could be avoided by the way of using the said feature. Hence I have structured a few more databases to organize the data which have made our works easier and also one could understand the same towards the tables which are given below.

Table 2.1.1 Single Model

Sl.No.	Mfn	Author ID	Sem.Mst	Output
1.	100	100	Saravanan T Dr	Saravanan T Dr
2.	101	101	Saravanan T Dr	Saravanan T Dr

Single database option has clearly explored towards the above Table from which you could observe that the author's name is entered two times in the IDs' 100 and 101 (Mfn-100,101) of the 'Sem' database so as the output would display the required data as it is. When we use the relational model we can get the same output but the processing of data would differ.

Table 2.1.2. Relational model

Sl.No.	Mfn	Author ID	Sem.Mst	Aut.Mst	Output
1.	100	100	Reference Link	Saravanan T Dr	Saravanan T Dr
2.	101	101	Reference Link		Saravanan T Dr

Look at the above table which has covered the details for the relational model, where one could realize that the author's name is not entered in the 'Sem' database and it is entered in the 'Aut' database only once. The relations are given in the 'Sem' print format commands by which the required author's name which is available in another database could be accessed. By using the relational concept, the same output which we have got in Table 2.1.1 could also be possibly shown in Table 2.1.2. The given diagram shows the E-R model concept.

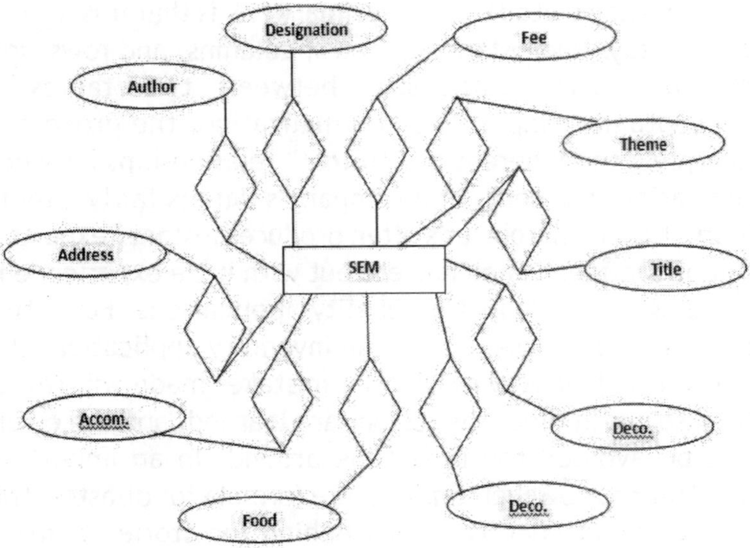

Screen Shot:2.3 E-R model

Even though the tables are independent, one can easily see that they are related. This relationship is the basis for the name relational model. This is the basic idea of a relational model. Data is stored in tables. They have the common type of information.

The relational model uses a collection of tables to represent both data and relationships among those data.

George Koch and Kevin Loney have pointed out the risks and dangers of relational models that the relational database tools will be as much as 20 times faster than traditional system development. And it will be very easy: Critics of the relational approach warn that relational systems are inherently slower than others, that users given control of query and report writing will overwhelm computers, and that a company will lose face and fortune if a more traditional approach is not taken. There are issues and risks that are brand new and not obvious. Once these are identified and understood, the risk is no greater, and probably much smaller, than in traditional development. Further they stated that the primary risk is that it is as easy as they say. Understanding tables, columns, and rows isn't difficult. The relationship between two tables is conceptually simple. Even normalization, the process of analyzing the inherent of "normal" relationships between the various elements of a company's data is fairly easy to learn. Unfortunately, this often produces instant "experts," full of confidence and naiveté but with little experience in building real, production quality applications. For a tiny marketing database, or a home inventory application, this doesn't matter very much. The mistakes made will reveal themselves in time, the lessons are learned, and the errors will be avoided the next time around. In an important application, however, this is a sure formula for disaster. This lack of experience is usually behind the stories of many project failures.

2.2. IDENTIFYING THE FIELDS

Identifying the required fields is perhaps an important task for any kind of database, as it is the backbone for all other processes which are going to be carried out in it. Careful attention and experience are a must to identify the required fields so that one could build a strong database to manipulate the data as per our requirements. Important fields shouldn't be neglected under any circumstances and it should be carefully analyzed before constructing a database. In contrary, no new fields shouldn't be included after the database creation as the newly added one might affect the indexing process as well as report generation. More experience is required to handle the said kind of action and avoid errors. Further, it requires a recycling process in the program sector (Format area) in which everything should be restructured. This is supposed to be one of the important processes that would definitely affect the data accuracy and maintenance. In that case, if any errors are committed by us in the format area, it has more validations that could be solved by us, when we have wide knowledge in it. Further, we have to check the data accuracy again from the first record onwards. This is not possible and it would consume too much of our time. This kind of job is an unwanted one, as we may be busy with our seminar work schedules and also it would not be a good data management system.

If you are an expert in WinISIS®, you may go ahead. You can add or delete the fields as per your choice at any time. For others who are not much experienced in WinISIS® better to avoid the risks.

So, capturing the required fields is an essential thing that should be carried out with full attention.

The following fields have been defined for the purpose of data manipulation in the *SEM* database.

Database: *SEM.MST*

Fields identified:

Id

Name

Desig (Subfields included)

Institution

Sex

Subfields: - Male

Female

Fee

Subfields: - Amount

Mode of Payment

Bank

Number

Date

Paper

Subfields: - Title

Abstract

Full Text

Aut1

Subfields: - Accommodation

Institution

Address

Certificate

Aut2 (Subfields included)

Aut3 (Subfields included)

Aut4 (Subfields included)

Aut5 (Subfields included)

The subfields identified from Aut2 to Aut5;

Name
Designation
Institution
Amount
Mode of Payment
Bank
Date
Address
Certificate
Accommodation

Reply (Subfields included)

Schedule

Subfields: - Facets/Themes
Press
Others

Accommodation

Subfields: - In charge
Contact No.
Locations

Acode
Dcode
Fcode
Gcode
Tcode
Index
Keywords

Attention: *Some of the fields, which have not been found in the FDT, could be generated towards the PFT data extract command option by defining the field's name as a label as it helped me to satisfy the local requirements. For* *instance, there is no individual field defined in the FDT for the e-mail id as this field is treated as one of the subfields of the field 'Aut1' and the mail id comes under the address and it has been labelled 'Phone/E-mail Id'. These kinds of features could be utilized as per our requirements wherever they are needed when we don't have such an individual field in the FDT. By way of defining PFT commands, we could manage our data beyond the limits.*

The given screen shot enables one to capture enough information about the fields which have been defined in the database.

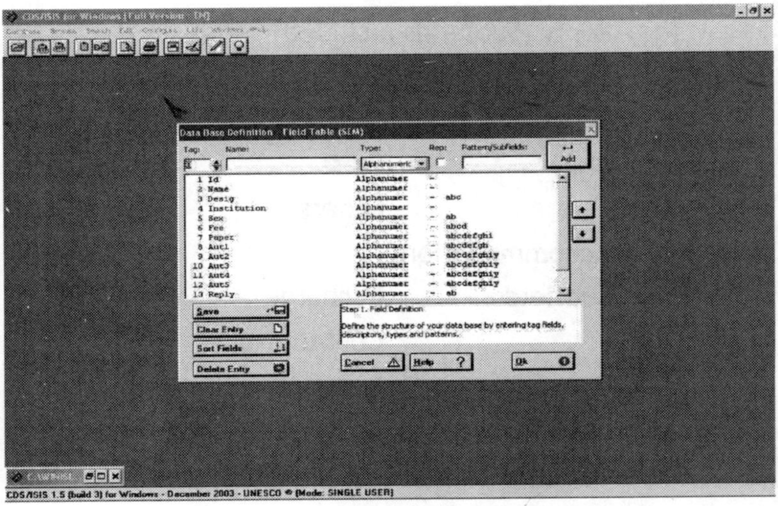

Screen Shot:2.1 Field Definition Table

2.3. FST DEFINED

Index acts as a key and enables one who is looking for the exact location of information. This is an important stage of any database that permits us to define the fields which help us to capture information in the database. Keeping these aspects in the mind, the indexing technique is applied for effective data searching. WinISIS ® offers wonderful indexing techniques from which we can opt our choices. In this database, I have opted for the following fields for the purpose of extracting data from the database.

Id

Name

Desig.

Institution

Sex

Fee

Title

Aut1

Aut2

Aut3

Aut4

Aut5

Reply

Certificate etc.,

The given screen shot enables one to capture enough information about the fields which have been defined for the data extraction purpose in the database. This option permits us to opt for the indexing technique at various levels for the fields which are selected from the FDT into FST, so as they could be captured towards the dictionary option while searching the data.

2.4. WORKSHEET

The worksheet is an essential item to feed the data into the database. This is also one of the features of WinISIS® that enables us to make our works so compact. A pick up menu has been structured for the required fields, wherever necessary. This option enables us to select the right choice and keep away from typing the data again. The typing errors could also be avoided when using this option. Worksheet includes many features that permit us to define the options which we would like to pick up during the time of data entry.

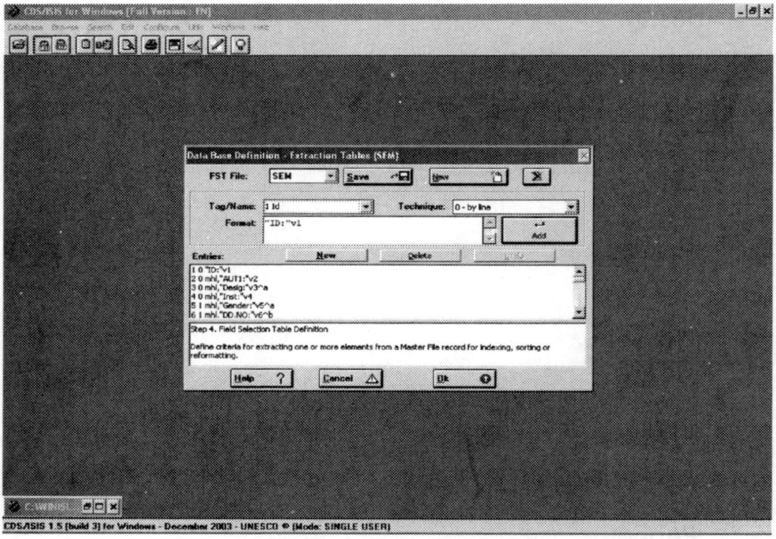

Screen Shot:2.2 Field Select Table

For instance, in the designation field, I have included some of the options that are categorized as given below:

The designations of the teaching professionals are classified as

Professor

Assoc. Professor

Asst. Professor

Reader

Sr.Lecturer

Lecturer

The designations of the library professionals are classified as

Librarian

Asst.Librarian

Library Asst.

Attention: Designation name may differ from location to location. You can opt the names of the designations which you have in your location.

The students' community are classified as

BLIS

MLIS

The Research groups are classified as

M.Phil

Ph.D

Like the above, fields Sex and Reply also have the said features. There is no restriction to define the pickup list for the fields. If you want to include this feature to some more fields that could be possible, if the fields for which you want to define must be deserved for that.

Attention: *As I have opted for the subfields procedure, which is quite familiar in WinISIS®, the data defining method could be properly handled so that they could be manipulated towards the display format. You can observe the pickup list entries from the given example.*

^Ph.D

^M.Phil and so on.

2.5. DATA ENTRY

A definition on data has been brought out by O'Brien

A.J., who states, "Data can be defined as facts, events or transactions that have been recorded. One of the important works in the database is data entry which needs more care at the time of the entry. These kinds of jobs could be done by an experienced person only. Having the knowledge of keyboard typing alone would never help anyone to feed the data in ISIS database as it has subfields and repeatable fields' and more that may or may not be found in some other packages. Hence fundamental knowledge in ISIS is an important thing to feed the data in it. More attention is required here as data entry plays the major role by which only the accuracy as well as the uniformity could be maintained. According to Wig K.M., information refers to facts and data organized to characterize a particular situation. The data entry worksheet related to the 'Sem' database has been depicted towards the given figure.

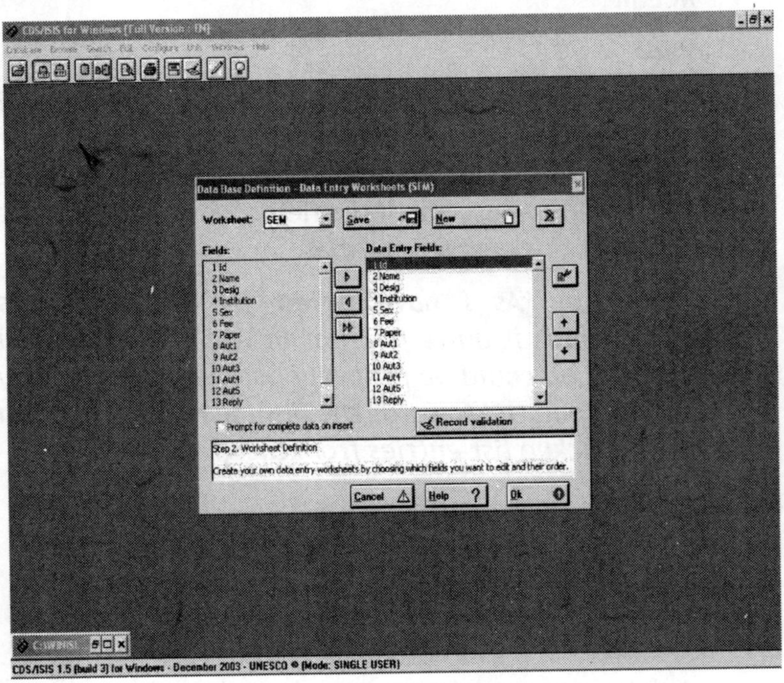

Screen Shot: 2.4 Worksheet

2.6. DISPLAY FORMAT

Print format is an important area in any kind of job. Like that the database 'Sem' developed by using WinISIS®, offers wonderful features by which the extraction of data as per our requirements could be possible. Defining different kinds of formats (ie: simple programs) only we can achieve the said outputs without which nothing would be possible. Simple but powerful formatting commands that are included by WinISIS® offer unbelievable features that enable the database designers to make their works easier, faster and more compact. I have ever seen such a wonderful package as it has sophisticated features in the database sector. I am fully satisfied when the said application has been utilized by me for the data organization in the national level seminar event. The tool which is behind the successful organization of the data and the outcome of compact seminar volume is none other than WinISIS®. The seminar volume includes more than 160 papers and 500 authors that include the co-authors also. The total record levels in the 'Sem' database has gone up to 206. The data display format could be viewed from the given figure.

The records level could be observed from the given figure that includes the option 'MAX: 206' at its right bottom. Further you could observe the full data distribution towards the screen shot and they have been explored clearly in the respective sub chapters.

It is one of the features of the WinISIS® Print format commands by which an access of a delegate visual could be made possible that you may observe from the above screen shot. The visual for the first author of the article could be viewed at the right top of the screen and the visuals for the rest of the co-authors if any that also could be viewed towards a separate window by clicking the option 'Show Picture' which has been placed near the author's details.

These features have been discussed in the forthcoming sections.

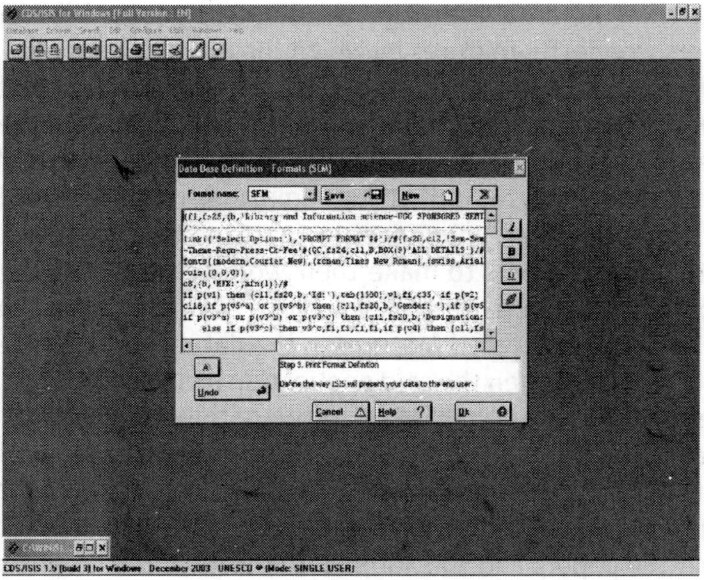

Screen Shot: 2.5 PFT

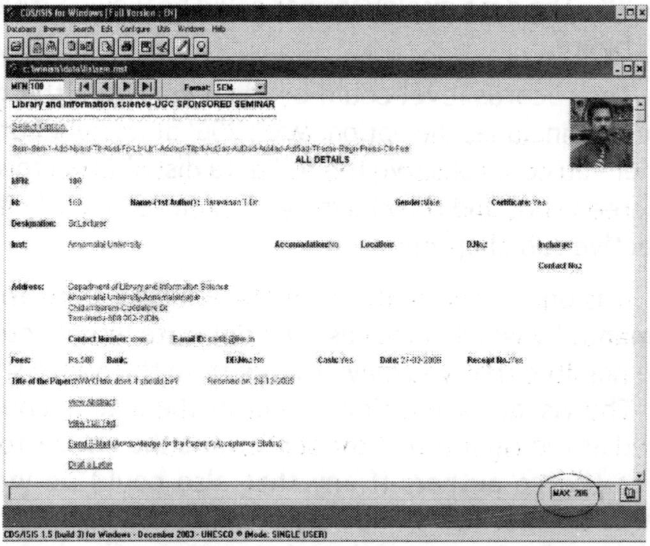

Screen Shot:2.6 Maximum Records Status

Attention: *It is a must to build a strong database before you start the data processing which is related to your tasks. Ensure the structure of database and enter the next chapter to carry out the rest of the jobs that might enable you to move your works in the right path.*

3

Data Organization

Abraham Silberschatz (et al) stated that data manipulation is;

i. The retrieval of Information stored in the database.

ii. The insertion of new information into the database.

iii. The deletion of information from the database.

iv. The modification of information stored in the database.

Further they pointed out that the E-R model is very useful in mapping the meanings and interactions of real-world enterprises onto a conceptual schema. The complete E-R diagram for the structured database could be observed from the *Annexure-i*.

This chapter gives enough information about the pre and post conference/seminar works which are to be taken to accomplish the task. After having a complete schedule of our program it is an important job of the organizers to disseminate information about the same to all groups of people who belong to this discipline as well as interested to turn up for this event. Pamphlets with the compact structure along with adequate details, such as title, areas, date, fee etc., may enable both of us to have a well meaning communication as well as understanding. The Abstract and Full Text of papers could be received via e-mail or in manual & electronic format by post as the editorial board has to do more scrutinizing jobs by which the said items may or may not be accepted. Once our desk receives the Abstract & Full Text format from the delegates whether it may be by e-mail or post the reply which includes the acknowledgement must be dispatched from our desk to the delegates at the earliest. Keep it in mind that we are not giving the papers an acceptance status at present. The reply has been given by us is concerned with the status of the paper whether it has been received by our desk or not.

3.1. AUTHORS' PROFILE

Once we receive the paper(s) from the delegate(s), enough bibliographical data should be carefully collected and fed into the structured database that could be observed from the given screenshot, where the sample bibliographic data of one of the authors has been displayed by which you can understand the further process. Here I have given the bibliographical data that is related to my profile that includes all details, and throughout this book I have used my data only for the sake of utilizing others' bibliographical data they may require prior permissions from the persons, whoever they maybe. Hence, I have not included any other person's details, which I have received to my desk, while I was processing the data for the seminar. Some of the data like bank, DD.No., accommodation, location, D.No., in charge, contact No., etc. are in blank as my bibliographical details do not belong to these categories Hence they have been left as they are. But, the persons who have the enough details could be viewed here that depends on the category of the users. Let me show the sample screen shot where you could capture my data.

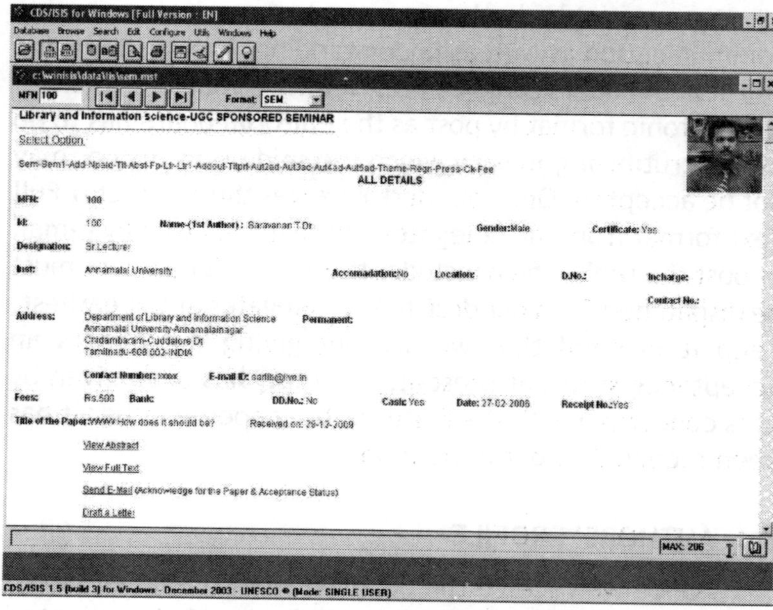

Screen Shot 3.1: Delegate's Profile

The delegate's profile along with the visual could be viewed from the above screen shot that is one of the features of the WinISIS®, and also this feature has enabled me to verify the author's identity, as and when required. Visual of mine could be viewed along with my profile. The details of the rest of the co-authors, if any, could also be displayed in the same method, and it has not been screened here, as I have already stated that it requires prior permission from the concerned person and that I didn't like to disturb others for this purpose as they may or may not be interested to offer their personal data.

Attention: *The first author visual has been viewed at the right top of the screen here and viewing the rest of the author's visual also would be possible in the separate window by clicking the required option which has been provided near the concerned co-authors. Equal weight has been given to all authors and not only for the first author.*

Provisions which are available for the first author would be also offered to the rest of the co-authors.

3.2. E-MAIL COMMUNICATION

One of the advantages of data management through this database is to have enough communication with the delegates as and when required without approaching for some other tools as WinISIS® offers full-fledged facilities to carry out our tasks from one place. In this connection, the reply must be given by our desk to the delegates, and it could be done by the given way, which has been clearly explored towards the screen shot, where you could observe more information about this process.

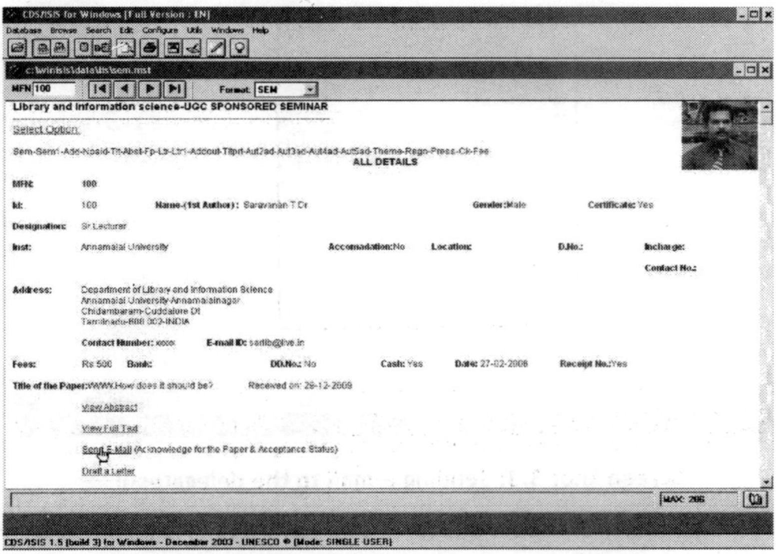

Screen Shot 3.2: Sending e-mail to the delegates-i

When you move the cursor on the option 'Send E-Mail' you would realize that the cursor will be changed from its actual shape that enables you to go further. By clicking this option you would be directed to the following screen shot, where you could observe that there is one e-mail window that would be displayed along with the delegate's e-mail Id, which has been captured automatically from the delegate's profile that could be possible by defining the print format commands. Ensure that your system must be connected with the internet before carrying out this task. This option helps us to send acknowledgement for the papers which have been received by our desk from the delegates. The same option could also be utilized to send the status of their papers whether they have been accepted or rejected by the editors' desk.

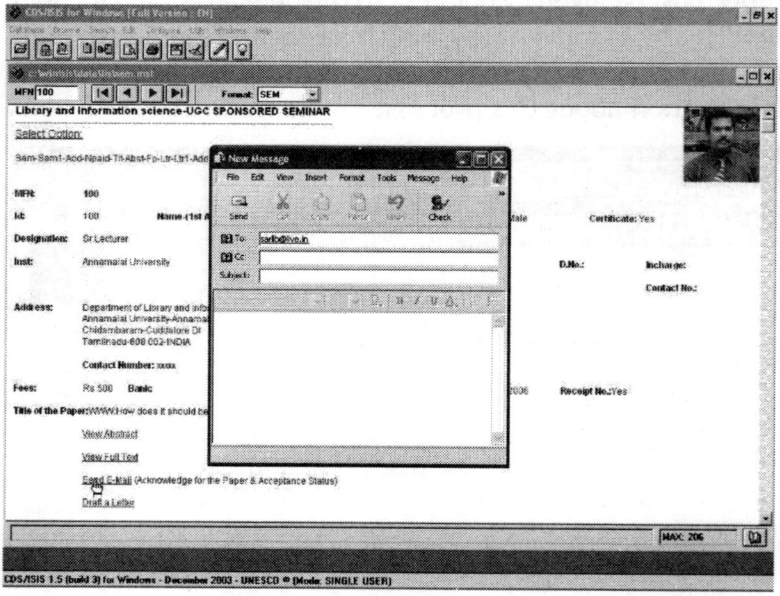

Screen Shot 3.3: Sending e-mail to the delegates-ii

The above feature makes our jobs easily by which we could communicate enough details at the moment.

3.3. POSTAL COMMUNICATION

The communication gap perhaps might be avoided under these circumstances. Keeping this aspect in mind, one more option has been structured by which we can send the communication to the delegate's address through post. Though we live in the technology era, postal communication is completely an unavoidable one. Hence, the facility also could be utilized by us for information transfer purpose. It is a wonder that some of the persons now-a-days are there without having an e-mail account or that account might have lapsed due to long gap of non operation. The senders some time may identify their e-mail id as wrong due to typing errors which we can see usually in many places. These are some of the reasons why we still depend on the postal delivery and for the same I have adopted this alternative letter delivery to our delegates. Both e-mail and postal to the delegates are always advisable so that we may avoid unnecessary queries from the delegates' desk, in case they would not receive the acknowledgement in proper time. The option named 'Draft a Letter' is available on the screen that could be viewed from the given screen shot.

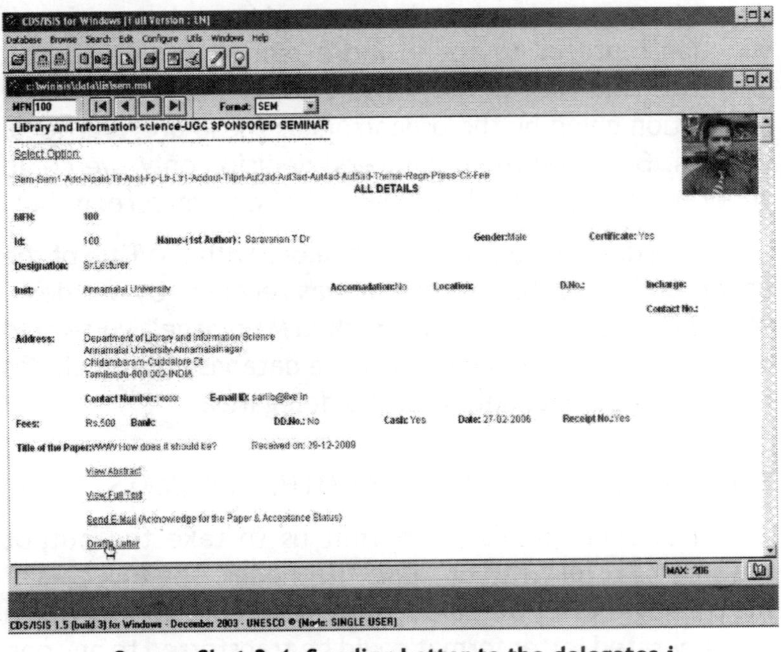

Screen Shot 3.4: Sending Letter to the delegates-i

3.4. LETTER OUTPUT TOWARDS DATABASE

When clicking on the 'Draft a Letter' you would be directed to the following screen shot where you could observe the pre defined letter format that could be printed towards the print option. Like that you can generate the output for all the delegates within the stipulated time. Observe that the delegate's visual is also available here for visual only and would not come for the print. The output starts from the 'To' address only as the report might be generated towards the letter heads so that I could avoid the 'from' option of this output. The delegate address would be captured from the database. So maintaining the delegate's address is an essential thing and any information which belongs to the address should not be left behind. In the above profile, I have given my office address only and did not include the permanent address. But provisions are there to generate the letter for their permanent address also that depends on your organizers' choice and financial position. If you don't prefer to spend more money for the postal purposes that may be avoided, else go ahead as per the instruction given by the organizers as these are your local choices. Based on the organizers' decision only, we could generate the output. Please observe the given screen shot.

The draft includes the letter along with the Title of the paper, and the date on which it was received by our desk. When you click on the option 'Back To Main page', you would be directed to the main form of the database that includes full bibliographical details of the delegates.

3.5. LETTER OUTPUT TOWARDS OTHER FORMATS

However, provisions permit us to take the output towards '.Txt' or '.Rtf' or '.Doc' file modes. The tool bars of the packages offer the said features (except .doc) by which the generated letter format could be transferred to any one of the file format that depends on our choice. If you prefer the menu based print option the said things are also possible. Make your choice. If you feel that handling the print option and other settings are not comfortable, you can prefer the tool bar methods to generate the output by the way of using the clipboard feature. Because, the margins and other settings are essentials in the print option, the sample output towards the textual mode has been formulated that could be observed from the given screen shot. For instance, I have converted the letter output from the database to the text file format. It is possible to convert the text mode to any other format and it is quite possible with advanced tools. For your information, I have generated more than 300 postal addresses within the stipulated time during the period of the seminar.

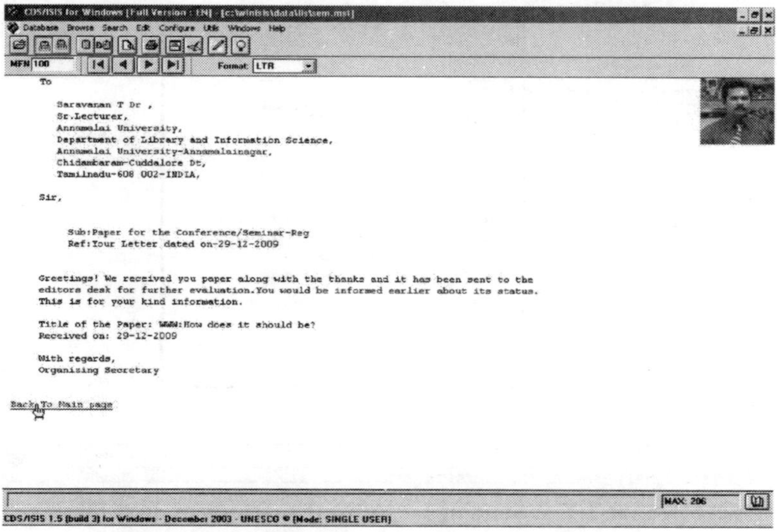

Screen Shot 3.5: Sending Letter to the delegates-ii

Remember that there is a problem while generating the address for the authors as many authors have the repetitions in some other records as first or second and so on. Hence the authors who have the same address should not be repeated again while taking the outputs. An author may come in three titles but he/she must be communicated along with the three titles to only one communication address and not to three addresses as the three addresses might be the same. Here careful process is required that enables us to keep away from wasting time, work and printouts. If you are not with care in this section too much of repetitions would bring unnecessary additional burdens to your desk that may damage your name among the authorities of the event who are behind it, as time plays a major role in all the events that should not be wasted under any circumstances and utilized carefully to keep the tasks in the right track so as we could get success in our jobs failing which could damage all works which you have on your desk since its beginning.

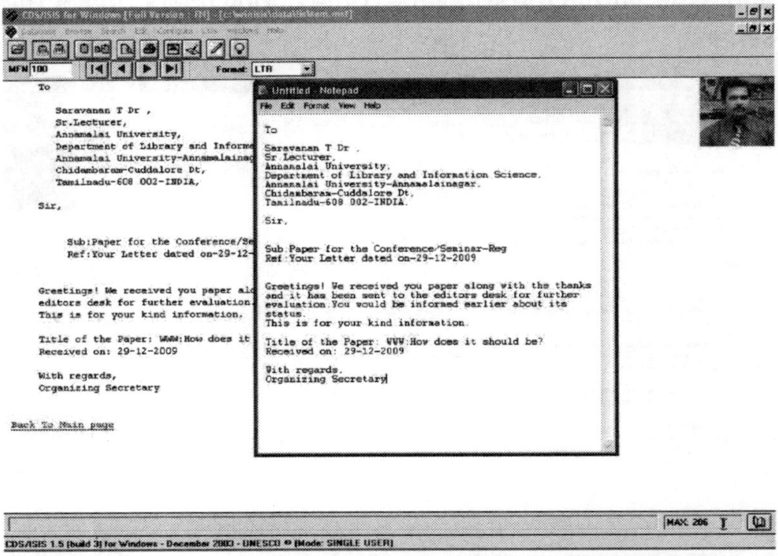

Screen Shot 3.5.1: Sending Letter to the delegates-Text File-iii

Attention: *See, it's human nature to degrade others when they get an opportunity and somebody is always there to blame your jobs whatever you have done. When you come forward to take such responsibilities don't forget that you must be ready to accept any type of comments whether they may be related with the encouragement of your works or* *discouraging ones. I have heard some things from the experts, which are unforgettable. Steven Spielberg who is the familiar director at an international level has expressed some notable words for the persons who are interested to work hard and come forward in their disciplines. "Welcome the comments from others and don't bother about them if the words are discouraging one." Like that I always welcome such comments to my desk and they would be accepted, if it is a healthy one or else rejected by my desk as too much of stress will spoil our works as well as health. If you are sure about your potentials, go ahead to accomplish the task which has been offered to you.*

3.6. PREPARING THE ADDRESSES

Let us have a look at the given screen shot that includes the details of the author who comes in two different titles with the same address. From the given screen shot, you might observe that the author who comes under the Id:100 is clearly explored within the oval shape along with the title of the paper and address to which the information should be communicated. The picture includes some of the details which have come under the oval shape for more understanding. They are;

ID-100

Address

Title of the Paper

You can compare the details of the selected author who has come in other places also with another screen shot that also has been visualized along with the said details here for better capture.

Look at the screen shot which is given below with the Id:101 along with the different title of the paper and the same address for the communication for the same author who has come in the Id: 100 of the screen shot.

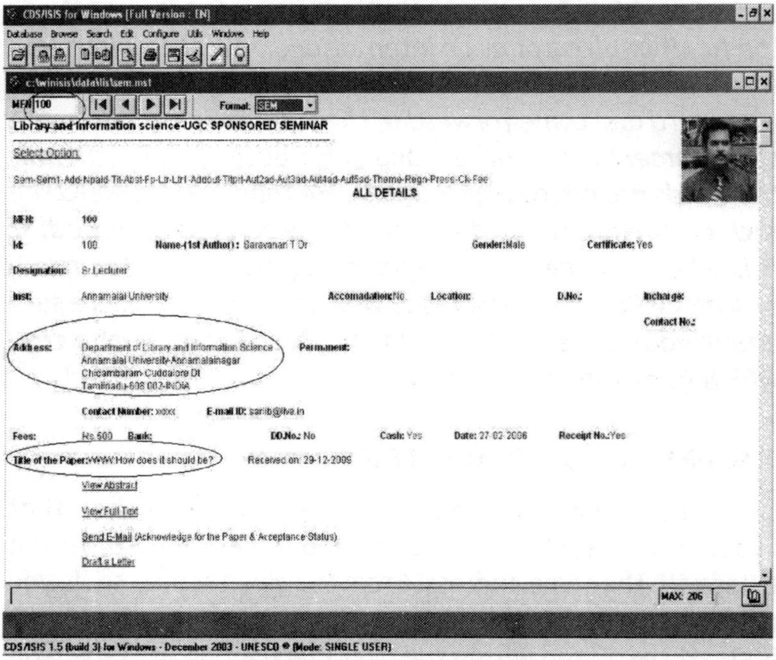

Screen Shot 3.6: Address of the Author with the First Title

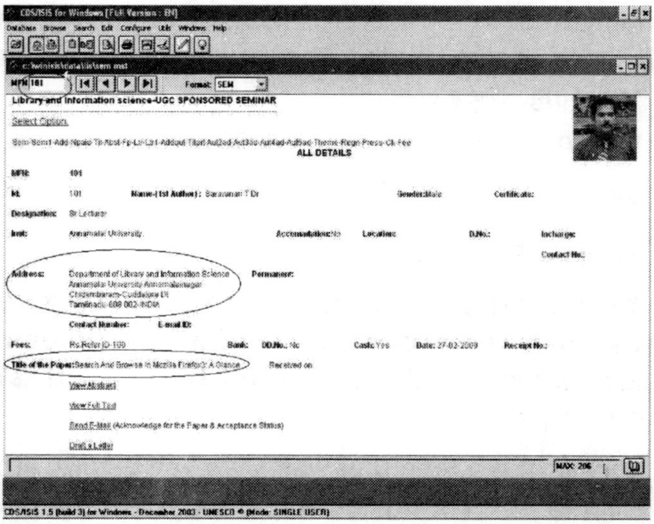

Screen Shot 3.6.1: Address of the Author with the Second Title

From both the screen shots, we could understand that generating two letter outputs are not necessary; instead of that only one output is enough to communicate.

3.7. SORT & PRINT: TEXT MODE

Here, I have opted the feature of sorting method of WinISIS® that enables me to generate the author's address in a specific sequence. Usually, the sequence might be in the ascending order. Print outs could be taken directly from the database. Though I have this feature in this database some other text editors are utilized by me to prepare the delegates address details. The data have been exported to the other files using standard conversion format and then stored in separate file for future reference. Further these types of generated output could be handled by any other person who is working for the event along with us with the little bit of basic system operating methods as they are permitted to take the printouts only. Also, this type of files handling would reduce our work burdens as they are all just printouts, which could be taken by any one as already said above. The method which has been acquired by me is handed over to someone for further process. The converted various formats of author address could be viewed from the given screen shots. The purpose of this output is that they might act as proof for the address labels that could be printed either ordinary paper or sticker featured papers.

3.8. SORT & PRINT: DOCUMENT MODE

The same output which is existed in the above screen shot has been generated again towards the document mode that is given below for your better capture.

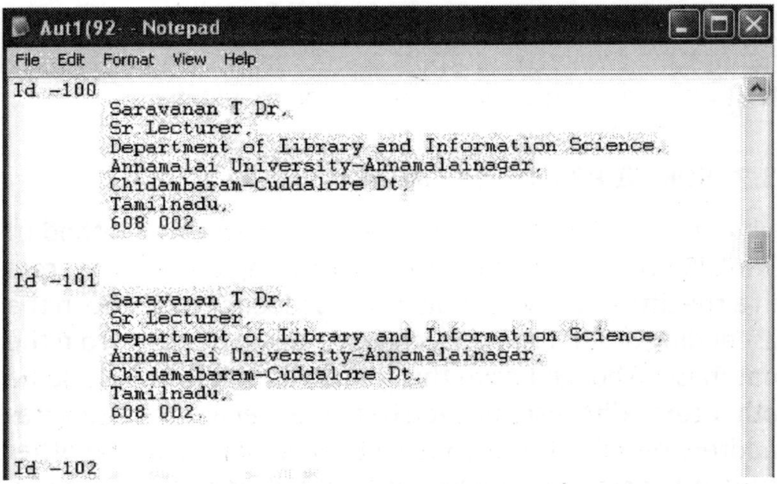

Screen Shot 3.7: Authors Details (Text file)

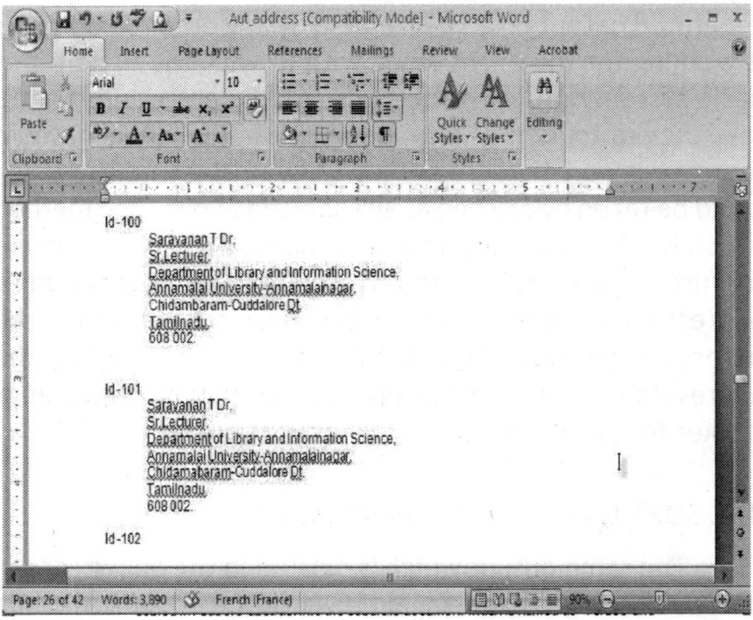

Screen Shot 3.8: Authors Details (Document)

The purpose of different outputs makes us to move our works with the required design. In textual format, there is no provision to set the font size and other attributes whereas in document mode all the provisions would enable us to modify the structure of the generated output as per our requirements. However, you can observe the repetition of authors' addresses who are the same. This output could be utilized to verify the papers' details along with the authors. Though the authors are the same, the title of the papers and other co-authors would differ. Hence, this kind of output with repetition is a must to have a cross check as and when required. Then what about the labels that should not have the duplication? Let us see the given screen shot where you can realize the extracted data output and this format may be used as labels.

3.8.1. Sort & Print: Classified Output in Text Mode

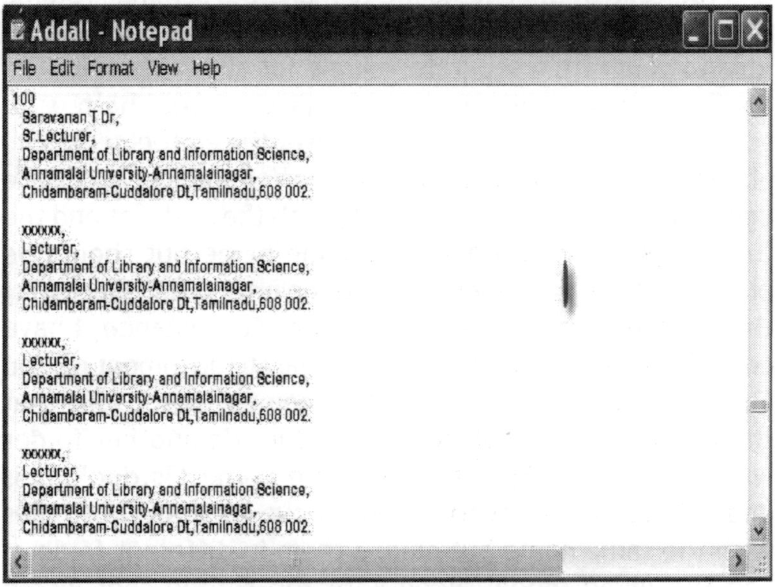

100
Saravanan T Dr,
Sr.Lecturer,
Department of Library and Information Science,
Annamalai University-Annamalainagar,
Chidambaram-Cuddalore Dt,Tamilnadu,608 002.

xxxxxx,
Lecturer,
Department of Library and Information Science,
Annamalai University-Annamalainagar,
Chidambaram-Cuddalore Dt,Tamilnadu,608 002.

xxxxxx,
Lecturer,
Department of Library and Information Science,
Annamalai University-Annamalainagar,
Chidambaram-Cuddalore Dt,Tamilnadu,608 002.

xxxxxx,
Lecturer,
Department of Library and Information Science,
Annamalai University-Annamalainagar,
Chidambaram-Cuddalore Dt,Tamilnadu,608 002.

Screen Shot 3.8.1: Address Labels (Text file)

In the screen shot, the author's address is explored along with the co-authors who have come for the same title. The Id:100 contains the address of all the authors (*co-authors names have been hidden here as already I said that it has been caused due to the non prior permission of concern co-authors*) for the particular title and towards the sorting procedure which is one of the powers of WinISIS® that enable me to generate this type of output where you could observe that all the co-authors are classified under the first author and not sequenced in alphabetical order as this sequence has been applied to the first author only.

3.9. PROCESSING ABSTRACT

Once the acknowledgement for the papers' works is over, the next stage would be waiting for us where we have to formulate the files as Abstract and Full Text. The purpose for which I have adopted the two way modes for the abstract and full text would enable me to make the seminar volume in a successful way. The organizers some time may have an idea to generate a separate volume for abstracts only. The above arrangements of the files system would help us to generate the required output whatever the editors seek. The abstract along with the Title, Author(s) and keywords are copied into a separate document. Both the abstract and the full text files should have the same name but should be placed in different folders to avoid the errors while accessing the files towards the database mode. For instance, I have copied my papers' abstract into a separate document named 'Ts.doc' and kept inside the folder named 'Abst'. Like that the full text paper has been placed inside another folder which is named 'Fp' under the file name 'Ts.doc'. It is understood that for every author, I have generated two files with the same name but placed them in different folders. See the given model along with the screen shot which includes the abstract and full text file access mode for better capture.

Abstract Destination: C:\DLIS\Sem\Abst \Ts.doc

You have your own choices to define the path of your

database as well as name for the external documents such as Word or PDF. Generally in any seminar/conference the instruction could clearly state that the delegates should send their abstract/full text towards the electronic format which may be in Word or PDF file format. I received the abstract/ full text in MsWord format from the authors via e-mail as well CD format by post. Defining the path for the database and other external files are an important task of the database designer so as the related works could be carried out without any risk.

Attention: *If you are an expert in WinISIS® application package the above said method could be possible by the way of handling the parameter files, in which you have to define carefully.*

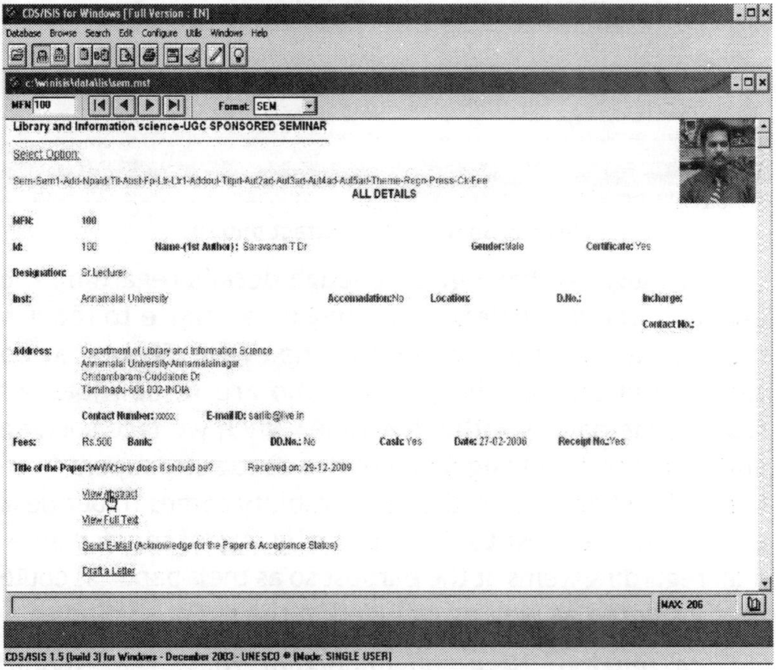

Screen Shot 3.9: Accessing an abstract

When you click on the option 'View Abstract' you will

be directed to the following screen mode where you could view the abstract of the select authors' paper towards the document mode.

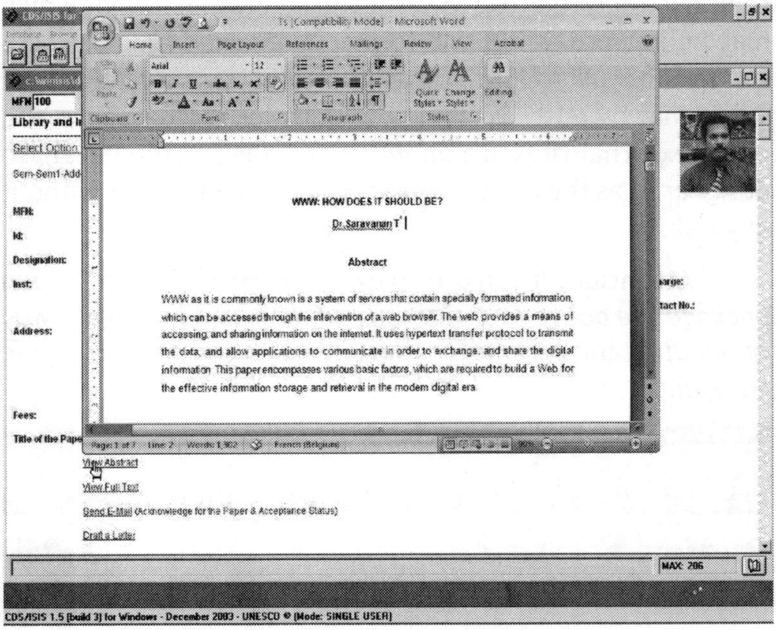

Screen Shot 3.9.1: Abstract output

Though we have given enough details regarding the papers in the pamphlets there may be a chance to receive the abstracts till the beginning of the event. There may be various reasons for the authors who are responsible for sending the papers within the time. When we face such an environment in getting delay of the abstracts/papers from the authors' desk, then the responsibility comes to our desk to make the request to the authors by way of sending an e-mail regarding items at the earliest so as their paper(s) could be considered as well as included in the event's volume.

Attention: *Here, an important thing that should always be noted is that the authors who have already registered only could be considered and their papers would* *be incorporated in the volume. Unless they have registered, they would not be considered and chances are there to exclude their papers from the volume also. However, by getting the assurance from the authors about their registration that may be done on or before the commencement of the event their papers may be considered and included in the volume that could be decided by the organizers' desk. If our desk receives the green signal from the organizers, we may include the paper that which has not been registered as on date.*

Some of the queries may be screened in front of your eyes while reading this section as;

Does the event prefer registration rather than the paper?

One could realize that the necessity for finance in any event which is to be expected to run successfully as the events are like a coin which has two sides and without any one side, the coin has no value. Like that, any event is depend on the finance, as it is the backbone of the event without which accomplishing the tasks are not possible for one and also they are painful jobs. The persons who have had any previous experience with the event organization could realize the said things as to how finance plays a vital role? How much trouble they have in raising the funds? However, having a wide discussion to raise the funds for any event is not discussed here as the main track of this book is not related with the finance and has been focussed into the data organization sector by way of using a rigorous tool.

3.10. PROCESSING FULL TEXT

Full text Destination: C:\DLIS\Sem\FP \Ts.doc

When you click on the option 'View Full Text', you will be directed to the following screen mode where you could view the Full Text of the select authors' paper towards the document mode.

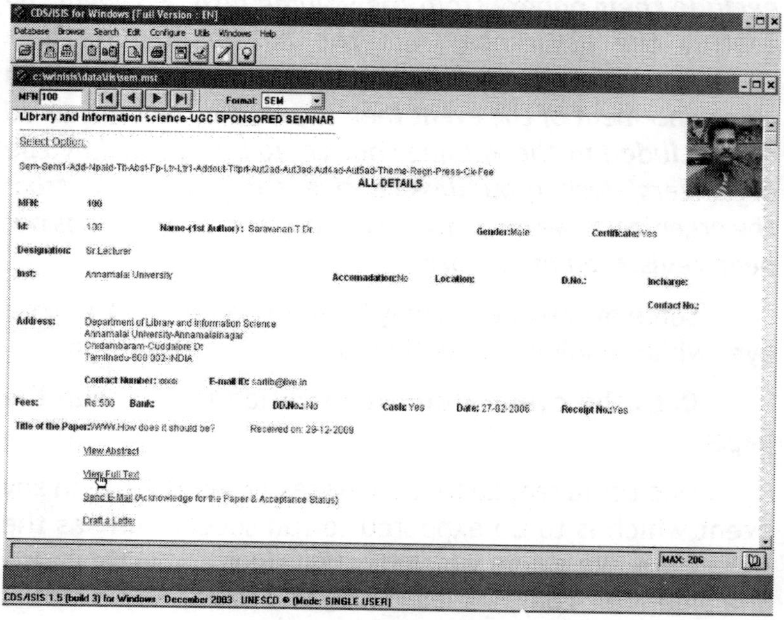

Screen Shot 3.10: Accessing Full text

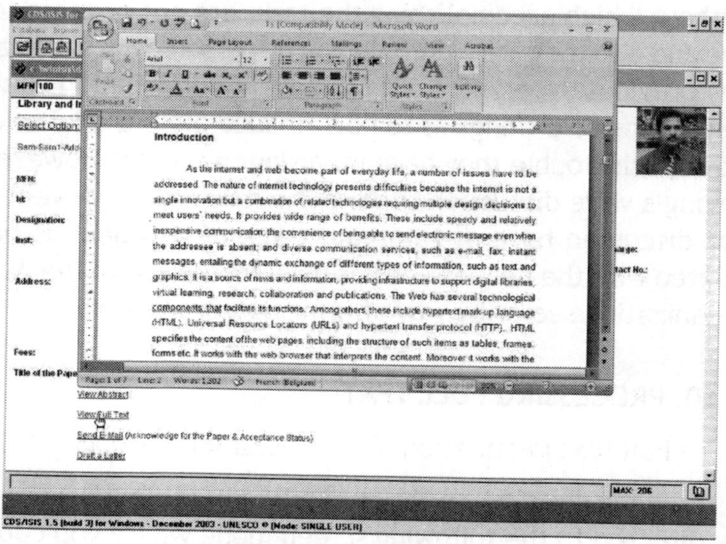

Screen Shot 3.10.1: Full Text output

You may define the method of your choice and adopt the first name or any other identification for the authors' papers. If you don't need to create the abstract file separately that could be ignored as it depends on your editors' choice. But having this kind of individual arrangements would definitely help us to compile the separate volume of abstracts, in case the editors' desk would have an idea about it. If you do these arrangements since the beginning of data processing, the burdens would be reduced from your shoulders. Imagine that you don't have an individual file format for the abstracts for all the authors' papers and you can generate the full text only at the time of compiling the conference/seminar volume.

If the editors' desk requires the abstract format alone at the last moment what will you do? Is it possible to process all the files within the moment? Of course, anything is possible with the existing technology, but here the important thing is we don't have enough time to process all the files as we are working for the event of a conference/seminar, which would not let us to consume more time. As a database organizer, it is our responsibility to capture any kind of information towards the structured database and they must be placed on the editors' desk for the next process. So, it is advisable to adopt two way file modes for the file organization whether the editors' desk could have the idea to publish the abstract volume or not. Ensure your side that your desk could have enough potential to produce any kind of output as and when required by the organizers.

I have included the provisions in the database to access the files which are available in '.doc' and '.pdf' formats. My paper has been accessed towards the document mode which you could see from the above screen shot. The authors' papers, which are available in 'pdf' mode, also could be accessed as some authors may prefer the file formats according to their own choice. Our next job is to transfer the received papers to the editors' desk as the papers require further evaluation for their potential and make sure that you have collected enough data from the papers so as they could be fed into the database for further manipulation.

3.11. COMMENTS FROM EDITORS' DESK

The Editorial board would carefully analyse the paper for its worthiness and they would pass any of the following comments to our desk that should be passed on to the delegates. Generally, the following comments would be expected from the editors' desk:

1. Paper is accepted.
2. Paper needs corrections as suggested.
3. Paper is too lengthy and it may be reduced.
4. Enough references are not found.
5. No standardization adopted to render the references.
6. Paper is not relevant to the subject.
7. Paper is rejected.

Attention: *The comments which would be generated from the editors' desk have been listed above, and there may be a chance to face some more comments that depend on the editors' desk due to local variations. As everyone knows that the editors' desk decisions are the final one and they should be obeyed by the authors whatever the comments may be.*

3.12. PAPER STATUS

You can use the mail option to communicate to the authors about the status of their paper along with the editors' comments, if any, which have been briefed above. Of course, this is an important task which must be handled carefully in our desk after the editors' desk process. The comments which we receive from the editors' desk should be passed on to the authors' desk without getting delayed so as the required corrections could be carried out by the authors, in case, if anything is notified by the editors' desk. Hence, the above works should not be held back to a latter time that may bring many problems to your desk. So do the jobs immediately within the stipulated time and have the evidences such as outbox mails and a copy of the drafted letter for the said communication that could be used later, if any, problems are raised from the authors' or editors' desk.

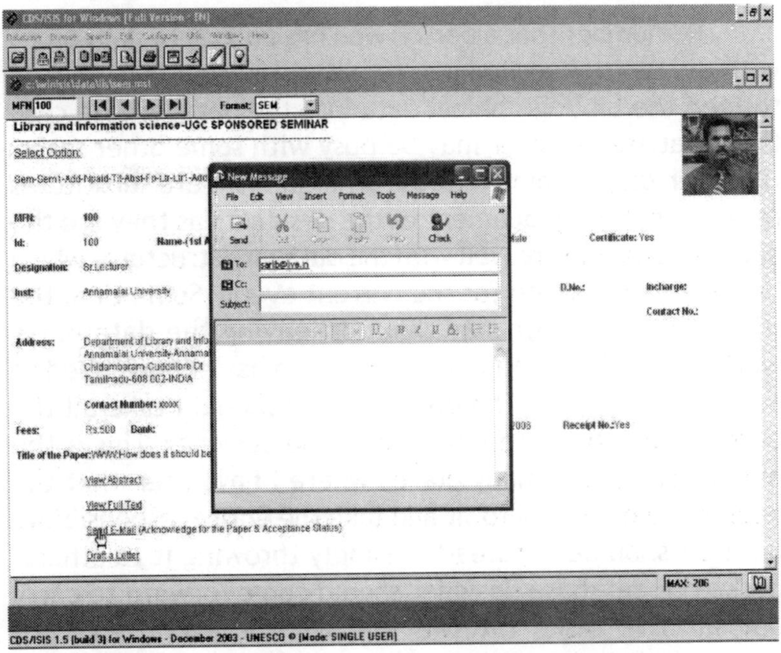

Screen Shot 3.12: Sending e-mail to the delegates-Paper status

The same communication may be sent by post to the authors' desk. The editors' desk has the complete rights to add any part into the papers or remove any portion from the papers. However, some of the areas that could be handled by the author(s) who is/are behind it by way of their tough expression. These kinds of barriers could be solved by the concerned author(s) only. When we face this type of environment, simply send the communication to the authors along with the comments which have been flowed from the editors' desk for further corrections to ensure the quality of the papers.

Because the editors' desk would always take care about the originality of the papers and its structure as any of the organizers who wanted to make their event as a good one compared with others as these events play a major role in the higher educational sector.

Remember that a person who has enough IT skills along with the typing knowledge is required and could be allotted to feed the bibliographical data into the database, in case the database designer may be busy with some other tasks. However keep in mind that the other persons are substitutes only and not a replacement of the designers as they are the only persons who are well with the database structure, which has been formulated for the current event. Some time the database developer may think of leaving the data entry works to the Data entry operators' who have been called to assist the designer. The question why should I take all the burdens may be raised in front of the designer. This is the major problem in many places where I have seen that the people are not ready to sit and take the entire responsibility on their shoulders instead of simply throwing it to others' desk. The database designer should come forward to carry out all the tasks till the end of the event and the responsibilities should not be transferred to anyone else under any circumstances so as the structured database could be effectively handled. The data entry operators may not be much familiar about the database which has been structured by us for the event. The entire structure could be easily understood by the person who is behind its development. We could expect the data feeding features only from the data entry operators that also may require a little bit of training before hand on the job as it requires uniformity and accuracy. Generally, the data entry operators are quite familiar with the text documents and not with the database records. Further, packages like WinISIS® requires compulsory fundamental knowledge and training in it so as data processing is possible or else it may lead to the unwanted errors that may bring more stress on us. We can't expect more from these kinds of data entry peoples that they will do a better job and satisfy our requirements. When the works are scattered to many persons, there is a chance to lose the accuracy as well as uniformity, which may cause too much of burdens to the developer shoulders, while generating the outputs. So keeping these things in the mind, I didn't let anyone to carry out the task in the database and all the works would be carried out by me as the application package requires experience to handle the data. Hence I myself sat in front of the desktop, even though I completed database creation and the works were done by me including data entry to maintain data accuracy and uniformity that would not be possible when we adopt someone else.

3.13. VALIDATIONS

The database includes provision for accessing the authors' visual that enables me to have a cross check not only during the time of data processing till the end of the event. Further there may be a chance to face the authors who are with the same name and in such a case these kinds of visual identification would make our validations easier and keep us away from getting confused.

Attention: *I got an opportunity to face the said environment while processing the data for the seminar event. I received three different authors with the same name and their identification could have been cleared by* *the defined visual option and realized that they were all different authors and not the same one.*

See the given Tables that enable you to capture some valuable information regarding the discussed environment.

Table 3.13.1 Different Author Validations

Sl. No.	Name of the Author	Mfn	ID	Authors' Place	Visual	Match
1.	xxxxx	120	120	First	Yes	No
2.	xxxxx	150	150	First	Yes	No

Column 1 shows the Sl. No.

Column 2 shows the Author's name

Column 3 shows the Mfn range

Column 4 shows the Author's ID

Column 5 shows the Author's location whether he/she is first or second author and so on.

Column 6 shows the Author's visual.

Column 7 shows the Author's visual match status.

Both the IDs' have the same author's name but actually they are different persons that could be traced via the visual identification.

Look at the table which is given below to capture more details.

Table 3.13.2 Same Author Validations

Sl. No.	Name of the Author	Mfn	ID	Authors' Place	Visual	Match
1.	Saravanan T Dr	100	100	First	Yes	Yes
2.	Saravanan T Dr	101	101	First	Yes	Yes

All the IDs in the above table deal with the same

author's name. In both the Ids, the author acts as the first one. The same author may or may not come in various records as he may or may not write the papers under various titles along with some other authors. Hence, possibilities are there to face the same author in various records.

***Attention** : If any mistakes are committed while entering the names of the authors or access link to the authors' visual which would bring more confusion to our desk as well as violate the data accuracy.*

Many of the authors, who have the role in some other papers have taken more than two places and some authors' role has gone to more than six to nine places as they have worked as a first or joint author in various papers. Simply, the same author has come in many other places as a co-author. So, there is a need to identify them with the different ID as well as with the visual.

3.14. RESTRICTIONS OF THE DATABASE

1. Database permits to add upto 5 authors' per paper. More than that would not be permitted as the database has no provision for that.
2. An author may act as the first or one of the joint authors. Concerned with the number of authors per title the decisions had been taken by the editors' desk. In my experience, I have seen that there is no uniformity adopted regarding the authors' collaboration per paper. Every organizer of the event has his/her own choice based on the authors' contributions.
3. For instance, an author has played a collaborator in more than 6 papers. Hence, I adopted the visual access option to identify these kinds of authors whose names are repeated again.

Attention: *My desk received various comments from someone regarding the joint authors count per paper and they were all ignored by me during the time of the event as i am not the authorized person to decide the boundaries for the authors count per paper. However, as a faculty member of the same discipline, i would like to express something which is concerned with the co-authors count. In one of the articles which was written by me for an international journal, I got an experience to analyze the conference paper* (Aziz, S. et.al.), which contained nearly 33 number of authors count towards collaboration mode. You could observe the said authors collaboration in a single conference paper, which is given below, and it shows that the collaborated research always moves on the right track that is a healthy sign in higher educational sector. More number of collaborations based on contributions is welcome at the international level whatever the discipline it might be. With the strong evidence any one can discuss with others when an opponent has only equal potential or else better avoid any type of conversations as it may consume your valuable time.*

Sample paper with 33 Authors contribution:

Accession number: 8082027

Title: A simulation of an event building network for the CMS high energy physics experiment

Authors:

Aziz, S. ; Berti, L.; Brigljevic, V.; Bruno, G.; Cano, E.; Csilling, A.; Cittolin, S.; Erhan, S.; Gigi, D.; Glege, F.; Gulmini, M.; Gutleber, J.; Jacobs, C.; Kozlovszky, M.; Larsen, H.; Litmaath, M.; Magrans, I.; Maron, G.; Meijers, F.; Meschi, E.; Murray, S.; O\'Dell, V.; Oh, A.; Orsini, L.; Pollet, L.; Racz, A.; Samyn, D.; Scharff-Hansen, P.; Sphicas, P.; Schwick, C.; Suzuki, I.; Toniolo, N.; Zangrando, L.

Year:2003

Document_type: Conference article (CA)

Publisher: IIIS

Material_Identity_Number:XX2004-00859

Author_affiliation:(1) Fermi Nat. Accelerator Lab., Batavia, IL, USA

Source: SCI 2003. 7th World Multiconference on Systemics, Cybernetics and Informatics Proceedings

ISBN:980 6560 01 9

Conference_name: SCI 2003. 7th World Multiconference on Systemics, Cybernetics and Informatics Proceedings

Conference_date: 27-30 July 2003

Conference_location:Orlando, FL, USA

Place_of_publication:Orlando, FL, USA

Sponsor:WOSC

(Source collected from INSPEC database)

In case if you don't maintain relational modal concepts, you have to repeat the data entry for the authors who are with the same name and you might be aware of the following things that enable you to avoid the errors at the time of the data processing.

Let us observe the given table which contains the authors' who are different, but having the same name. For instance, I have given my name here for better attention.

3.14.1. Space between the words

While feeding the authors who have the same name and occur in different records, I have committed a typing error due to duplication. Look at the given table where you could view the authors' name and how did they have been entered in the record.

Table 3.14.1: Dictionary Term

Sl.No.	Name of the Author	Dictionary
1.	Saravanan T Dr	1
2.	Saravanan T Dr	1

Please note that in the first row two spaces are found in between the name and the initial of the author and the same has been entered without mistakes that could be observed towards the second row of the Table. The required output of the above data should be displayed in one time but due to typing error the author's name would appear twice in the dictionary window. Remember that both the author names refer to the same person.

3.14.2. Missing entries

Table 3.14.2 Missing entry status

Sl.No.	Name of the Author	Dictionary
1.	Saravanan T	1
2.	Saravanan T Dr	1

Some more kinds of data entry mistakes are explored towards the above table by which you could understand the need of care while feeding the data into the database. See that the author's higher qualification is not found along with the author's name in the first row of the table and the same has been entered with the additional data that could be observed towards the second row of the Table. The required output of the above data should be displayed at one time but due to the errors committed as stated above, the author's name would appear twice in the dictionary window. Remember that both the authors' names refer to the same person. It is a must to keep the data entry with full care to avoid the said instances till the end of the event.

3.14.3. Punctuations

In all the cases, I have avoided to use the punctuation marks such as '.' ',' etc, as the package offers wonderful features to include any of the punctuation marks with the data output by way of defining simple programs which are referred to in the print format. Any other databases, in which you prefer to organize your data also has the said features only when you could interact with the database directly towards the concerned queries that may or may not be done by way of using the front end of the commercial packages and also you must ensure whether these kinds of features are predefined in it or not. If you do not prefer the front end access and interested to work directly with the database the said options are possible by writing your own queries only. Let us observe the given output where you could capture more information.

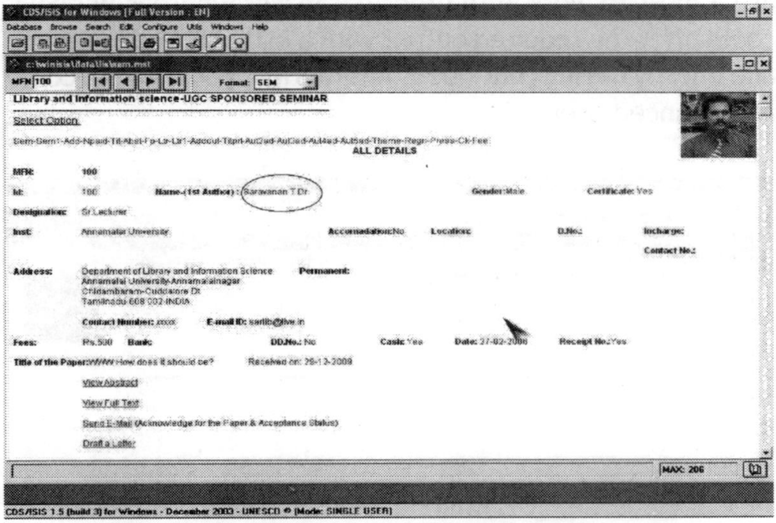

Screen Shot 3.14.3.1: Without Punctuation

From the screen shot, you might understand that the Name (1st Author) does not contain any punctuation. if required, punctuations could be inserted in between the words as per our requirements; if there is a need, that could be viewed from the given screen shot.

Look at the above screen shot in which within the oval shape you may identify the punctuation in between the name, whereas the screen shot 3.14.3.1 has not included the same that would be possible towards the print format commands which are available in the WinISIS® application package. Data extraction is a compulsory one in any kind of data processing and this feature enables the data organizers' desk to accomplish their task without much burden. Such a sophisticated tool I have never seen in my experience though I am interested in some other databases like Ms-Access® and Oracle®. I am not comparing any one here. Because of the features of WinISIS®, I was attracted by the package. At the same time, the other databases are also stronger in their own way. But advanced skills and experience to define the queries are a must to work with other databases whereas WinISIS® could offer the required output with a little bit of experience and only by having continuous interaction, you could become an advanced user.

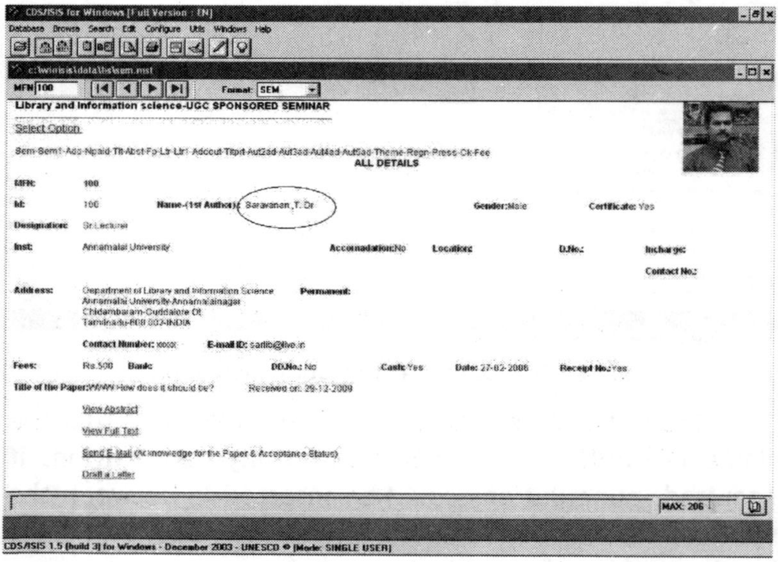

Screen Shot 3.14.3.2: With Punctuation

3.15. CONFERENCE/SEMINAR REGISTRATION

In all the conferences/seminars, there is no exemption for registration fees and these are regular routines. The fee structure could be decided by the authorities of the event.

The process which I have acquired to organize the fee details for the authors would give more information to you.

3.15.1. Delegates & Fee (Indian currency) Structure

The different categories of delegates have various fee structures. The delegates are classified as

a. Staff

b. Scholars

c. Students

Each category contains its own sub divisions that could be traced towards the field's identification which has been discussed in the previous chapter.

Like that, fee structure also has been categorized according to the delegates' category and they are explored as given below:

a. Staff -Rs.500

b. Scholars -Rs.300

c. Students -Rs.200

It is a must to fix the structure of the delegates and fee before processing the data with any of the database. Hence the pre defined conditions are carefully validated and the required print formats are formulated to generate the required outputs. The Complete details regarding the fee should be sent to the authorities' desk as well as the finance committee desk so that they could carry out their tasks as they are the persons who maintain all income and expenditure of the event.

3.15.2. Mode of Payment

Database includes the feature to extract the payment details with the required data. The fee may be paid by Demand Draft or Cash or by any other accepted mode. In all the conferences/seminars, usually registration through the cheque is not accepted. So, the bibliographic details of the D.D or Cash Receipts should include the following information as they may be required to take a cross check at any time. The data which could be gathered from the D.D or Cash Receipts are;

a. Amount
b. D.D Number
c. Receipt Number
d. Name of the Bank
e. Branch
f. Date
g. Mode

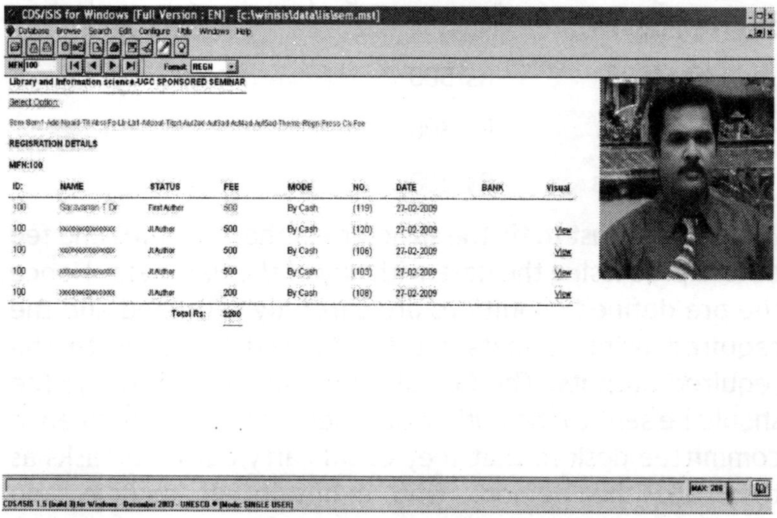

Screen Shot 3.15.1: Registration details

Enough details have been explored towards the above screen shot regarding with authors' registration. Each column is clearly explained one by one for better understanding.

3.15.2.1. Fee

The authors who are displayed in the above screen shot have made their payment by cash mode; hence the column 'Bank' is shown as blank. If the payments are made through Demand Draft then the required details would be captured in the area bank. The authors belong to staff category and so they have paid Rs.500 towards the registration fee that could be clearly identified from the given screen shot.

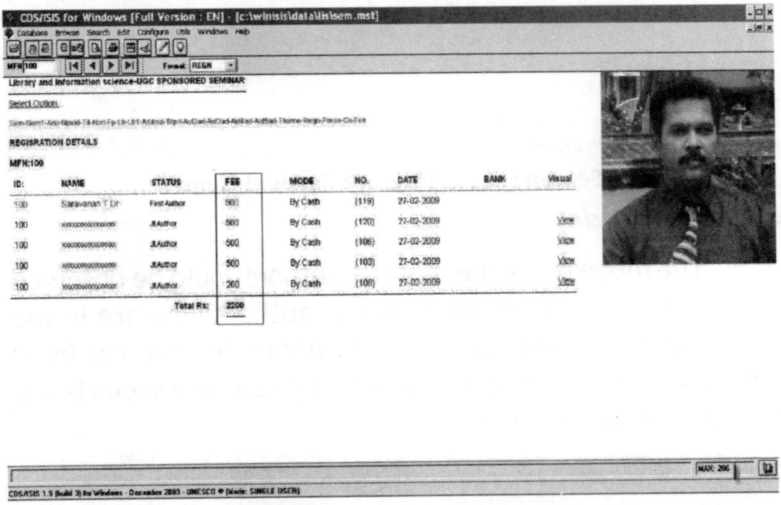

Screen Shot 3.15.2.1: Fee

Further, the screen shot enables you to observe the registration details for the Id:100 that shows all the information concerned with the authors, fee, mode of payment, no., and visual feature. You could further observe that there is no need to use any separate tools to calculate the collected fee as all the databases having the provision to add or subtract or multiply and so on. In the same way, WinISIS® includes the feature to sum the values that make our tasks easier. The sum of the fee for the displayed authors for the specific id also has been included in the generated output that could be observed from the next screen shot.

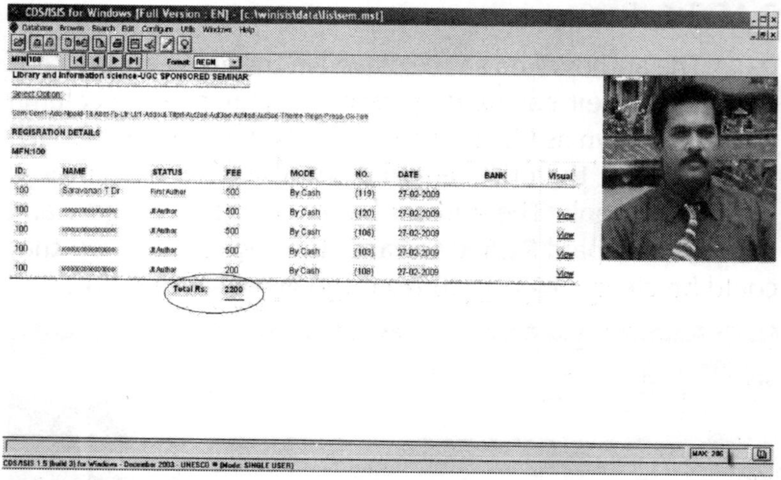

Screen Shot 3.15.2.1A: Fee with sum

3.15.2.2. Mode

The mode of payment of the authors could be observed from the given screen shot. As the authors who are in the Id:100 belong to the same faculty hence the fee has been paid by them through cash mode and it could be seen clearly in the concerned figure.

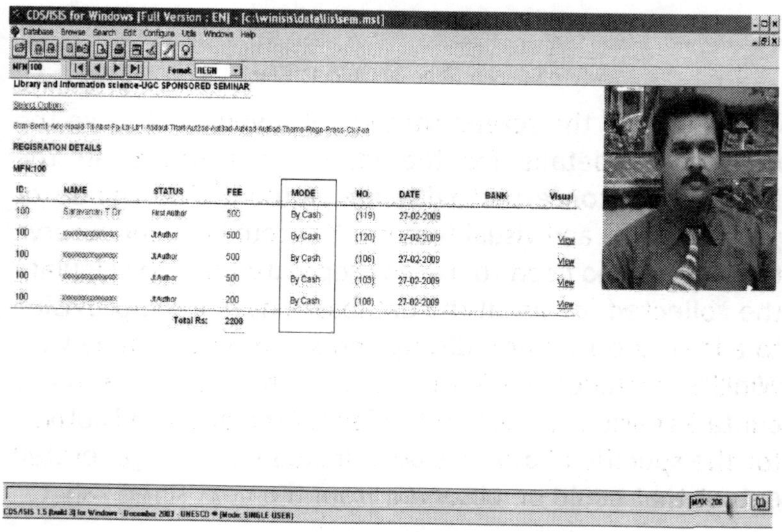

Screen Shot 3.15.2.2: Mode

3.15.2.3 D.D/Receipt Number

As the numbers are essential identification whether the mode of payment is by D.D or cash receipt (for the persons who would like to pay by cash directly), it could be observed from the screen shot which is given below. The spot registration method also is usually available in the system in which the receipts would be issued on payment of the fee that has been clearly discussed in the concerned forthcoming chapters. This section requires more attention while entering the unique numbers for the Demand Draft or Receipt as they would cause a number of problems along with confusions that would have been discussed in the next sections.

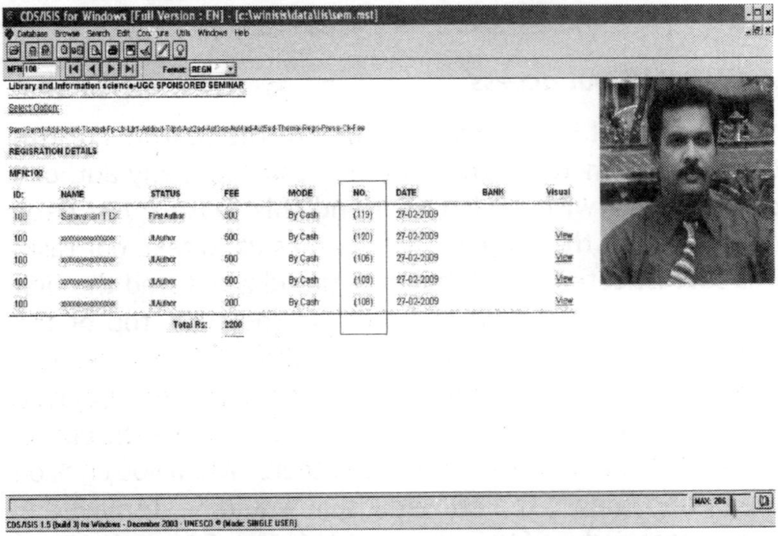

Screen Shot 3.15.2.3: Number of D.D or Receipt

3.15.2.4. Bank Details

As already discussed, the authors who are displayed in the given screen shot for the specific id have made their payment by cash mode. Hence the column 'Bank' is shown as blank. If the payments are made through Demand Draft, then the required details would have been captured in the area 'bank'.

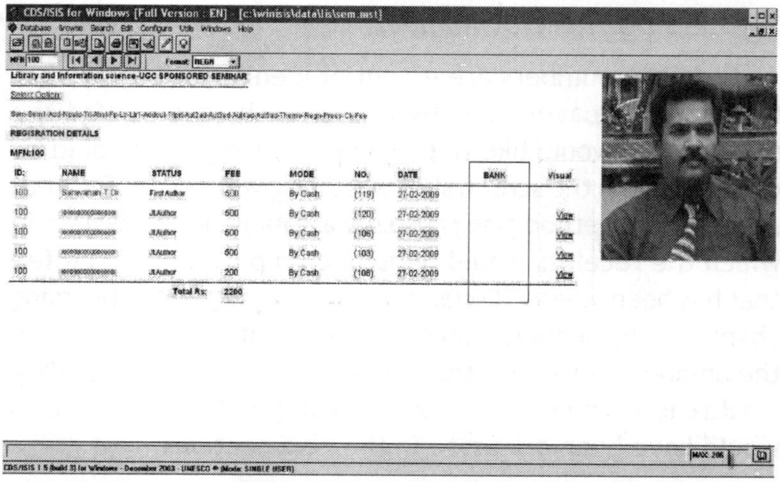

Screen Shot 3.15.2.4: Bank option

3.15.2.5 Visual access

As visual identification is one of the features of this database, it includes the provision to access any author's details along with their visual and this feature has been adopted in all the outputs that enables us to take our tasks in a sophisticated way. Whenever the id is entered the first author visual would be explored on the right top of the screen whereas the rest of the co-authors' visuals could be accessed by way of clicking an option that has been displayed towards the given screen shot where you could see the option 'view' opposite to the concerned authors. When you click on the option 'view', the related visual would be displayed in a separate window if the image exists in the right path. Visual identifications are the features offered by modern technology that could be properly utilized to carry out our tasks. The authors may be requested to send the paper along with their visual in the electronic format preferably, 'JPG option'. In this database, I have included the provision to access the visuals which are available in 'JPG format' only and the other formats would not be traced as I have not opted for the provision to trace the visual format which comes in the format other than .JPG. The size of the .JPG format is also space consumable where as other formats such as .BMP etc could take more size. Let observe the given figure.

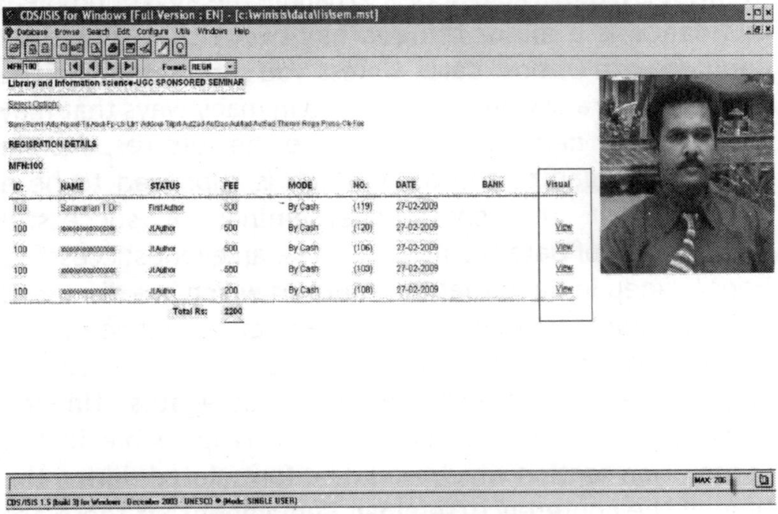

Screen Shot 3.15.2.5: Visual option

3.15.3. Validations in Registration

It is the best way to send the D.D to the desk of the finance committee or concerned authorities to whom it should be sent after having fed the required bibliographic data. Don't keep the items on your desk unnecessarily that may cause problems to you in case of their missing. Attention also is required to enter the D.D number or receipt number without committing errors, as they are an important task which without having cross checks may lead to wrong data retrieval and you might fail to maintain data accuracy. It is advisable to have multiple verification on DD/Cash details with the display which has been generated from the database before finalizing the registration tasks. This kind of process would allow making corrections, in case any errors occur.

Both the system and manual checking are essential as well as unavoidable routines even if there is a need to spend more time to take them. When this process is missed by us definitely it will cause problems at any time when they have some errors in them. When the persons are busy with the event, it is a tough kind of task to handle this kind of problem as finance is a major thing in any event that should be handled with utmost care. Unless you sure about the fee details, accuracy would be suffered in many ways that may damage your name also as your are the sole responsible person to organize the data which is supposed to be a backbone of the conference/seminar. A successful organization of data is a must to make an event successful. Hence, keep in mind that the routines which are discussed here shouldn't be omitted under any circumstances. The wrong registration data organization would be a problem not only with us but it also affects the delegates, finance committee and the persons who are responsible in the registration section which would be formulated during the time of the conference/seminar. Remember that these are like chain process in which if any one of the stage gets the error the other stages would also be hanged. The entire work fully depends on registration without which organizing a function is a tough task. The delegates may not have enough time to have a cross check with the database as well as with the in-charge of the registration counter, as the delegates may be busy with their paper presentation and other related things. So, keeping this aspect in mind the registration details should done with more attention so as these kinds of unwanted circumstances would be neglected, and bring peace not only to our desk but to all. Because, when organizing such a big event, it is quite natural to face any one of the problems. So, it is the duty of the concerned in-charge to try to do their level best. Just imagine the environment when your desk is surrounded by more number of delegates due to registration errors which have been committed by your desk at the neck of moment during the event. Luckily, I didn't get this kind of problem as I myself took the validation in the registration part not only that entire parts were under my control as I didn't prefer someone else to handle the tasks. For instance, observe the given table that shows the fee details with errors.

Table 3.15.3.1 Right entry

Sl.No.	Name	ID	Author status	Fee	DD/Receipt No.
1.	Saravanan T Dr	100	First	500	119

Table 3.15.3.2 Wrong Entry

Sl.No.	Name	ID	Author status	Fee	DD/Receipt No.
1.	Saravanan T Dr	101	First	500	1199

An author who comes under the IDs 100 and 101 have paid the amount of Rs.500 or 300 or 200 that depends on their category by the way of receipt mode and the receipt number for the first author is identified as 119 that is clearly explored in the first table. At the same time there was an error that occurred in the second table that shows the receipt number as 1199 which was caused due to the typing error accidentally. See both the authors' names refer to the same person and hence the receipt number must also be the same. These types of errors occur that would not match the data at the time of the cross checking of the receipts. The duplicated entry also would be created in the dictionary that causes the confusion as the receipt number may or may not be issued to someone else and the person may belong to any of the category. This is violation of the data accuracy and reliability. What would happen when one searches the data for the receipt number 1199? Look at the given output.

Search Term: Receipt No.:1199

Output:

Record 1:

ID	: 101
Name	: Saravanan T Dr
Designation	: Staff
Fee	: 500
Receipt no.	:1199

Record 2:

ID	: 201
Name	: xxxxxxxxx
Designation	: Scholar
Fee	: 300
Receipt no.	:1199

In the above output, record 2 has the accuracy and the correct data is retrieved towards the search term as an author who comes under the Id: 201 might have the receipt number 1199. Because of our mistakes the receipt number has been wrongly issued to the Id: 101 where as the author's actual Id is 201 with the receipt no. 1199 and not 101 with 1199 that yields the results of wrong output. Further you could observe that the Id 201 falls under the category of scholar whereas Id 101 is belonging to staff category. The fee structure for both categories would also differ. These are the violations of the data entry system that would not let us to retrieve the right data.

According to Abraham Silberschatz (et al) the cardinality ratio of a relationship can affect the placement of relationship attributes. Thus, attributes of one-to-one or one-to-many relationship sets can be associated with one of the participating entity sets, rather than with the relationship set.

***Attention:** Here, the Id concepts which I have acquired could be understood by persons who have the fundamental knowledge of the database and its related concepts. For others or beginners would get too much of confusion and it is better for them to have good experience before entering any of the database concepts. It is advisable to handover the conference/seminar data organization works to persons who possess enough skills to carry out the tasks with technology.*

3.16. FEE REPETITIONS

As I have already discussed in the previous sections, an author's name may come in many records as first author or co-author with different titles. However, we can't claim fee for all the papers wherever the same name comes. Any author usually pays the fee at one time. Let us observe the given tables that contain fee details of the author.

3.16.1. Fee for the same author: Wrong Entry

Sl.No.	Name	ID	Paper	Fee	DD/Receipt
1.	Saravanan T Dr	100	Paper 1	500	119
2.	Saravanan T Dr	101	Paper 2	500	119
	Total			**1000**	

In the above table the author who comes in various records with the different titles has paid Rs.500 as registration for towards the receipt which has the unique number 119. In the Id: 100 we have entered the fee as 500 and the same has been repeated in the Id: 101 also and it leads to the error in the output. When the sum function used to calculate the total fee received the output for the above table must be,

Total : Rs.500

And not,

Total : Rs.1000

The above table might give the output as Rs.1000 for the fee which has been collected from the author id: 100 and this is a wrong data entry and validation. If these types of errors are repeated in many records wherever the same author comes there would be a big variation raised concerning with the income and expenditure areas. These kinds of errors must be avoided to ensure the accuracy in order to maintain quality of the data organization.

3.16.2. Fee for the same author: Right Entry

Sl.No.	Name	ID	Fee	DD/Receipt
1.	Saravanan T Dr	100	500	119
2.	Saravanan T Dr	101	Paid	119
	Total	**500**		

The above table clearly shows the corrected data entry method in the fee sector where it should be carefully adopted.

I have included the validation in the database to exclude the said type of errors and the given screen shot may bring more information to your desk about it. The screen shot shows bibliographic details of the fee for the authors who come under the Ids: 100 & 101, where you could see that the data are blank and it is assumed that they have already paid the fee under the id:100 that could be observed from the previous screen shot.

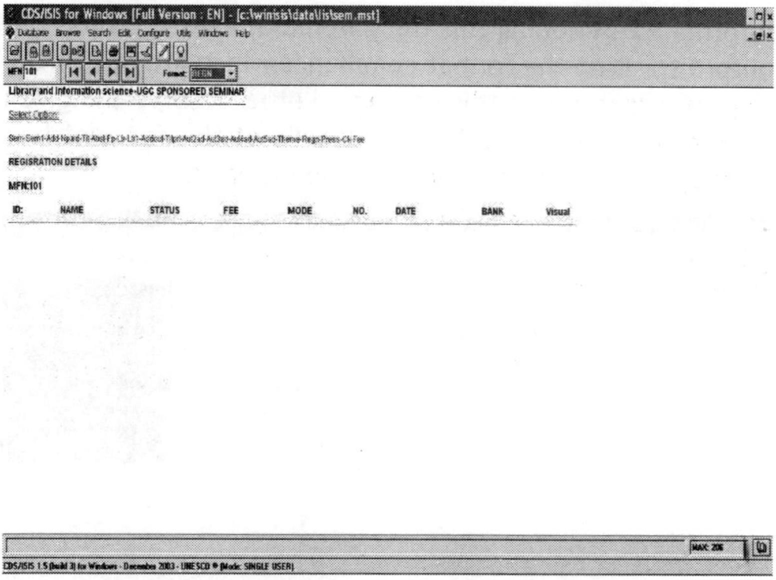

Screen Shot 3.16.2: Fee for the same author: Another record

However, accessing the screen like above is not a good one and it must have some details without which the purpose of the database would not be fulfilled. Showing the blank screen would not help us to capture more information and from the screen shot we trace that the authors have not paid the fee. The above screen just shows the Id and the column labels only. The purpose of any of the database is to retrieve much information to the designers as well as others. Unless we utilize the features of the database not only in WinISIS®, but in any kind of application, our tasks would not be accomplished as well as the goals of the packages would not be satisfied. Simply any observer of the screen without reading the previous sections might think that the fee has not been paid by the authors and they would not realize that they have already paid the fee and the related details could be retrieved from the Id:100. How do they know about it? Hence it is better to make our screen with some adequate data than as blank as it would help us to capture and retrieve more information. Keeping this thing in mind, I restructured the output by using the format commands which are one of the powerful features of this package. Let us observe the given screen shot that includes the details of the fee which is already paid by the authors in some other id.

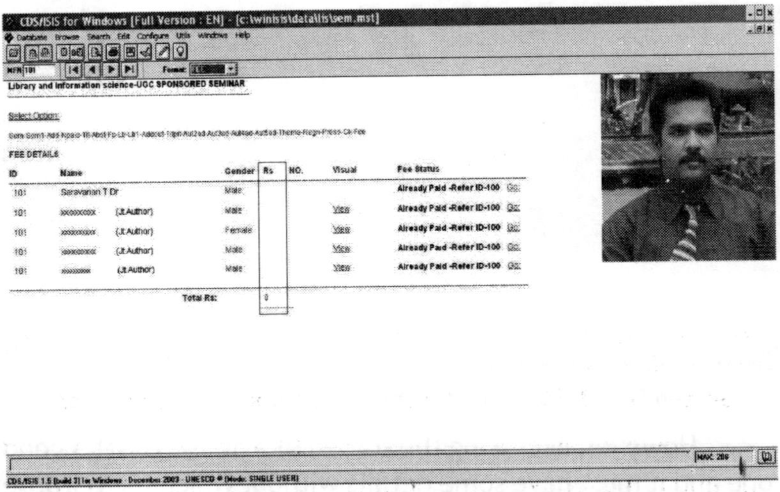

Screen Shot 3.16.3: Fee: Already paid details

In the above screen shot, you could see that there is no data displayed under the column 'Rs.' as the authors have already paid the fee and the required details have been stored under Id:100. If the same fees repeated in id:101 also, it would be the violation of data accuracy and its reliability also would be questioned. Hence, to avoid this situation, the output has been generated by defining the format commands of this database with full care. You might observe the sum also here, as it is denoted by the value 'zero'. It is better to compare the display where the same authors have come along with the fee details. Look at the given figure and compare it with the screen shot 3.16.3.

From the given screen shot you could observe the display 'Already Paid' that enables us to understand the payment details for the concerned author.

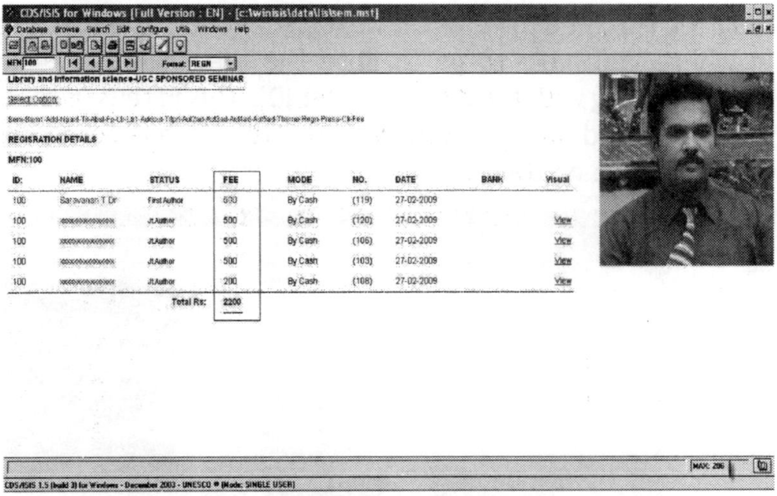

Screen Shot 3.16.4: Fee: Already paid details (repeated again for comparison)

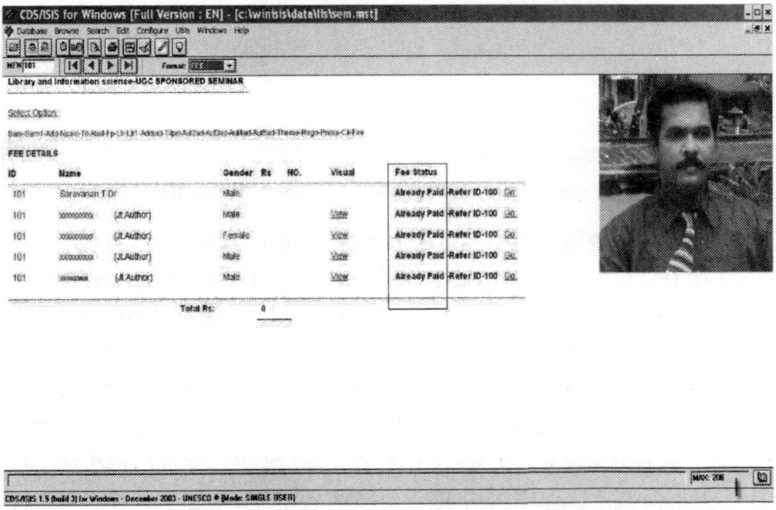

Screen Shot 3.16.5: Fee Status: Already paid

Further, the features to trace the specific id in which the authors have paid the fee could be included in the database by which the above screen shot has been formulated where you could see the display 'Refer ID' that has been explored towards the next screen shot. The specific id where you have to go to note the fee details is also included along with the display 'Refer ID'. This id tells us that the concerned author along with the fee details could be browsed if we go there.

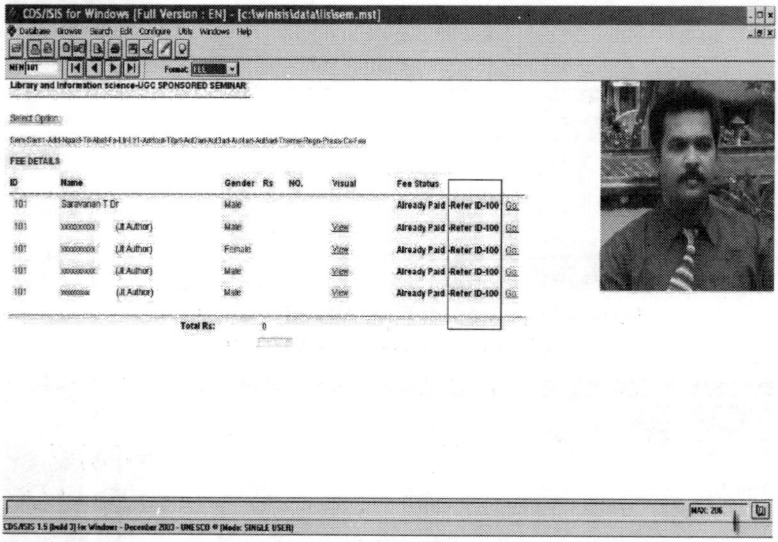

Screen Shot 3.16.6: Fee Status: Refer ID

A single screen shot offers multiple features that enable us to carry out multitask as per our requirements that could be realized when you work with this database. The authors who come under the Id:101 have all paid the fee and the required details exist in id:100. But this is not the same for all other authors who come in many places as they may have fee details in various Ids like 50 or 81 or 91 and so on. The display of the 'Refer ID' option which exists in the above screen shot would not be the same for others as they may or may not come in the continuous Ids. The purpose for which this feature is included here is we could trace the fee details for the specific author without moving from the screen to the next one. We need not apply any search terms to locate the author and fee details, as this screen offers the features and reduces our burdens also to go for the search options and apply a set of key terms, etc. Let us observe the screen shot where you could find the option 'Go'.

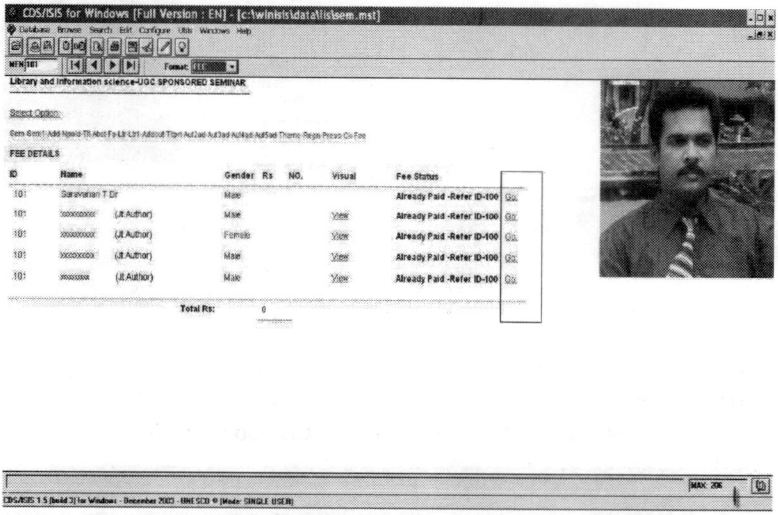

Screen Shot 3.16.7: Fee Status: Go

The cursor would be automatically changed while moving it on the option 'Go'. When clicking on the option 'Go' an option would appear where we have to enter the specific id for further process. Observe the given screen shot that contains enough details about the process which are explained here.

After entering the Id, press the 'return key' that would take you to the specific id with which you would like to go to access more details. The screen shot which you have accessed from the above screen shot is shown here. Observe the difference between the two screen shots that the above one is related with the Id:101 whereas the given one locates the Id:100.

The provision to access the user's visual on this screen shot is also explored here. We should not suffer in getting any kind of data; hence visual features are also included.

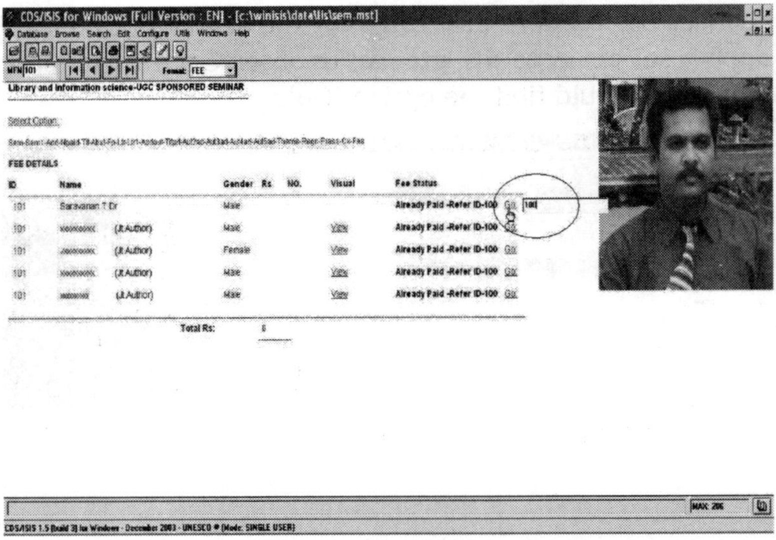

Screen Shot 3.16.8: Fee Status: Go with ID

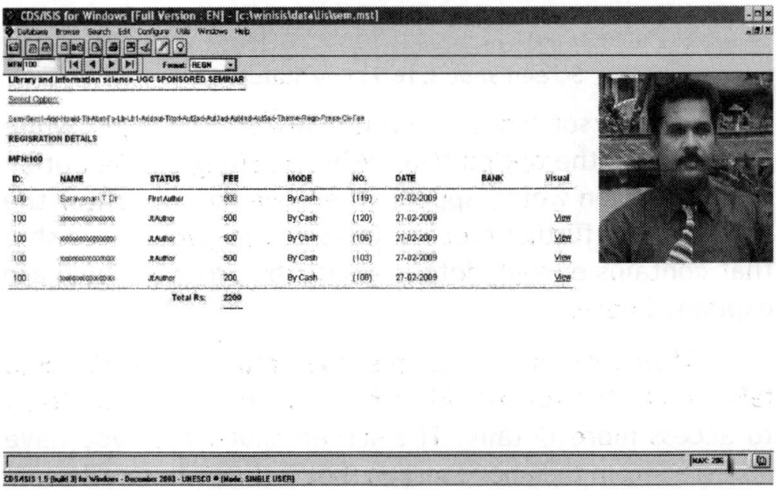

Screen Shot 3.16.9: Fee Status: Accessed from the option Go with ID

Attention: *We can build the database to maintain the data before the event has commenced, as we have enough time to structure it. But receiving the data from the authors' desk might be finished within a short period. Though we have announced the last date to send the papers* *to the editors' desk, there might be a chance to receive the papers till the beginning of the event and this would happen due to the local variations. When the editors have an idea to bring out the conference/seminar volume, the data processing works should be completed within the stimulated period so that the press peoples could carry out the printing tasks. So, unwanted things such as data repetitions, typing errors wrong entries, etc., could be avoided to speed up the process. It is an essential work to search the author for the duplication whenever we receive the papers from their desk as we have to structure their data in a standard format so that consumption of more time would be avoided. We should not forget to check the author visual also at the time of feeding the data into the database. For instance, I receive more than six papers from an author on various dates. In such circumstances, to group all the details under a single author is a major task that requires the above said formalities to confirm its identity or else more number of duplications would be created that should not be allowed.*

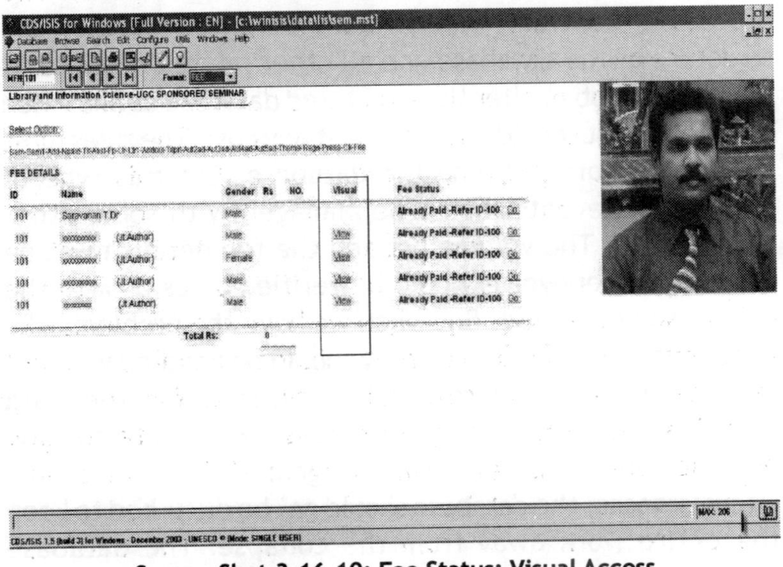

Screen Shot 3.16.10: Fee Status: Visual Access

3.16.3. Papers without Fee

Sometimes the delegates may give an assurance about their registration as it will be paid on the spot. In such a case, the organizers would have to take the decision whether to accept or reject their papers for the presentation as well as to include them in the volume. This type of environment is purely a local variation, which should be faced by any database organizers. Hence, it is an important factor, which I want to bring it to your notice that you could structure your database with full compact mode. I opt for the provision in the database which is structured for the said event to exclude the papers from the volume when they would not have the registration details. Note that their papers are permitted to come for the presentation as they have given the assurance to the organizers. Hence, I have not included their details in the volume part whereas the presentation part might have it. I received the direction from the organizers to include the paper(s) in the volume list, even if the concern authors have not done the registration. The process is contrary which would definitely violate the structure of the database and all other related routines. It is a difficult job to alter the structured database as and when required and it should not happen at any cost. The rules must be clear before defining the database. But this type of unexpected events should be managed with some other alternatives. The volume list and the fee details must be matched, whenever it would be verified by us or with the help of someone else. But when we have the problems like the above discussed things, they should be handled with full care as we are the responsible persons for the data organization. Whatever the database we create for any purpose, one thing can never be ignored, i.e.; under any circumstances, the database should not be disturbed to keep the entire work away from the collapse. The database constructions are already finished and the time which we have on our desk would only let us feed the data and process them only. In the middle of the jobs within the short duration, that may be a week or month, the validations could not be restructured, as there may or may not be a chance to commit the errors in the programme sector as we might have a tight schedule that would not let us consume more time to carry out the additional tasks which have been discussed above. Hence, it is advisable not to modify the defined structure, which may lead to many problems in data organization. If you want to take the risk to modify the structure, take the backup of your database as it is and then continue if time permits. I do not prefer the restructure option instead of that I have used some other text editor tools to maintain these kinds of details whereas the actual database is maintained as it is without violating the structure. The data which violates the structure of the database is identified and maintained in a separate file format. Though these are dual jobs, I have taken the responsibility and had more attention when I was working on it.

Attention: *Remember that we are not the decision makers concerned with the fee, registration etc. We have to obey the command which flows from the authorities of the event. Whatever the package you have on your desk to process the data, keep it in your mind that the real time process always differs, when compared with the theoretical sketch. Whatever the rigorous blue print we have on our desk that may or may not be blocked at any one of the places by the said violations that could not be avoided, which may be caused because of certain local variations. Because, the rule is register first then come for the presentation. Based on that rule the database would be structured by us. If it is broke what the database organizers would do? Though I am a qualified one in the database sector I do not attempt to restructure it as I have the short span of time to complete* *the tasks. Hence I decide to opt for the alternatives which have been discussed before.*

3.16.4. Multiple Authors

When we have more than one author for the title the validation must check all the authors' fee status and based on these things the paper would be included in the volume list after having scrutinized the paper that could be carried out by the editors' desk. For instance a paper has five authors. The program would analyze the fee status of the first author and include the authors' details along with the paper into the volume list as well as presentation. The same process would be carried out to the second author and goes up to the end of the co-authors that depend on their count. Remember if any one of the author among the five has already registered his/her details it must be included into the volume and the presentation list, even if the rest of the authors who may be first or co-authors have not done their registration previously. We could not expect that all the authors for the paper would register simultaneously. They have their own time and to register within the deadline and if the rule permits they may come for on the spot registration that is quite natural in any event. But we can't assure them that their papers would be included in the volume that the decision would be taken by the authorities.

Attention: *Remember that it does not mean that the authors who have not paid and also joined as co-authors with someone who has already done his/her registration, are permitted to attend the event and become eligible to receive the kit that includes the volume, certificates, and some other important things. The authors who have not previously done their registration may come for spot registration and they have the rights to claim the kit and other things. So, more care is required to exclude any of the authors from the volume, and other things are listed. If we* *fail to carry out this kind of things due to our poor attention, the authors who have done the registration would be suffered and also there are possibilities to relax the authors who have not done their registration. Such kinds of confusions should not be raised under any circumstances as it could be solved by our successful data organization only.*

3.17. PROCESSING PAPERS

The structured database includes all the features to store the bibliographic details of the received papers, such as title, authors, abstract, full text and so on. Observe the following screen shot that includes all the data.

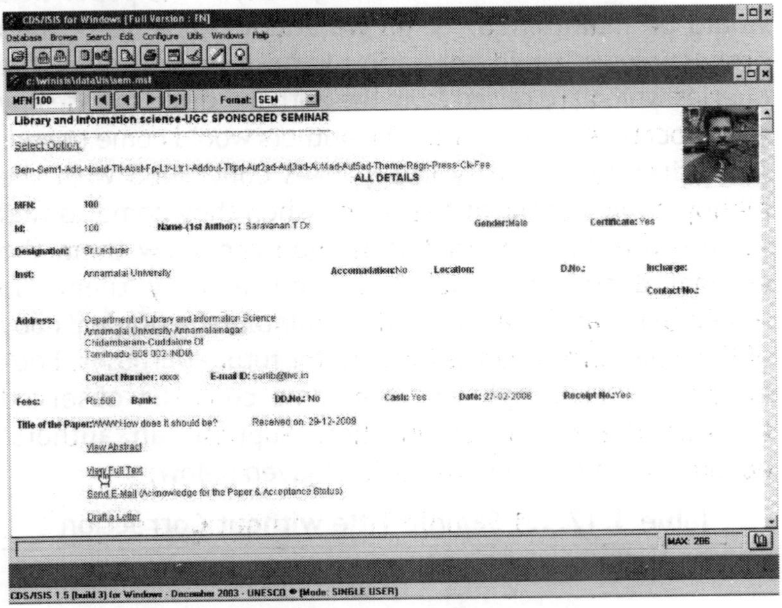

Screen Shot 3.17.1: All details

An important thing which I would like to note down here is the data entry for the said items. Better to avoid typing the data of the title, authors, institution etc. and instead of that, you can follow up the given steps.

3.17.1 Capturing Title

Open the document which has been sent by the author and select the title first and change the styles, if any, such as bold, italics, underline, caps, etc., into normal format. Better to use the same font and size for all the data. Now copy the title of the paper and back to the database to paste the copied items in the predefined area. This process would help you to keep away from typing the data and also from committing the typing errors. When I started the process, I used the typing method and realized soon that it was not comfortable and also time consuming; hence I adopted a revised style by the way of capturing the data from the author's document so that the originality of the paper title would be maintained. When we adopt this kind of data processing we would not be in the position to answer the queries which are raised from the authors' desk, in case any errors occurred in the title. The authors would come to your desk directly to clarify the queries concerned with the bibliographic details of the paper when they come to find some errors in it. At that time, you can show them the original document which has been sent by them. So remember that there is a need to maintain the original copy of the paper in a separate location for future purposes. Look at the given example and the same could be observed towards the given screen shot. Suppose an authors' document may contain the title as given below;

Table 3.17.1.1 Sample Title without Correction

Sl.No.	Title
1.	*WWW: HOW DOES IT SHOULD BE?*

Or

Sl.No.	Title
1.	WWW: HOW DOES IT SHOULD BE?

The above title format could be changed as given below so as the uniformity could be maintained to make the output as good.

Table 3.17.1.2 Sample Title with Correction

Sl.No.	Title
1.	*WWW: How does it should be?*

Or

Sl.No.	Title
2.	WWW: How does it should be?

But, the format should not be like as given below.

Sl.No.	Title
1.	Www: HOW Does it should BE?

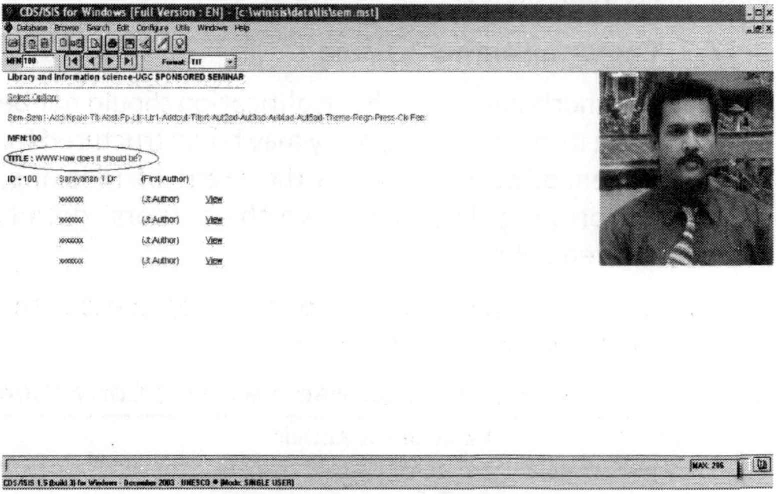

Screen Shot 3.17.1: Title format

The above format which has been changed from its original format would look like simple one and this kind of format may or may not be adopted throughout the records in the long run. The adoption of the format styles depends on your desk. The format which is shown above would have been adopted by me in the structured database to maintain uniformity as well as accuracy.

Attention: *Abraham silberschatz and others have noted that a relationship set is a set of relationships of the same type. Formally, it is a mathematical relation on* $n \geq 2$ *(possible nondistinct) entity sets. If* $E_1, E_2 \ldots E_n$ *are entity sets, then a relationship set R is a subset of* $\{(e_1, e_2, \ldots, e_n) \mid e_1 \in E_1, e_2, \in E_2, \ldots E_n\}$ *where* $(e_1, e_2, \ldots e_n)$ *is a relationship.*

If you are familiar with the database designing, you may use E-R model (see Annexure-i) for data maintenance and this is the only way for the designers to save their time, energy, storage space etc., otherwise you can use the simple data entry model to organize data. But, remember that this process will require the repeated data entry for the same data. Make your choice.

3.17.2. Capturing Author's Name

The author's name and the qualification should not be changed from its originality but they may be restructured for our convenience, particularly, in the areas of indexing, sorting and printing. Let us observe the authors' details which are given below.

An authors' document may or may not contain the author's name as given below.

Table 3.17.2.1 Sample Author Name without Correction

Sl.No.	Name of the Author
1.	*Dr. T. Saravanan*

The above author's name may be converted into the format as given below that enables us to process the index and other sections of the database as well as to ensure uniformity.

Table 3.17.2.2 Sample author name with correction

Sl.No.	Name of the Author
1.	Saravanan T Dr

The same method should be applied to the co-authors also, if any, along with the first author. Now copy the author's name and past it in the database, where it has the exact location.

3.17.3. Capturing Institutions

The name of the institutions in which the authors are working could be captured as per our need. Let us observe the authors' details which are given below:

An author's document may or may not contain the Institution's name as given below:

Table 3.17.3.1 Sample Institution without Correction

Sl.No.	Name of the Institution
1.	*ANNAMALAI UNIVERSITY*

The above author's name may be converted into a format as given below that enable us to process the index and other sections of the database.

Table 3.17.3.2 Sample Institution with Correction

Sl.No.	Name of the Institution
1.	Annamalai University

Table 3.17.3.3 Sample Location without Correction

Sl.No.	Name of the Place
1.	*ANNAMALAINAGAR*

Table 3.17.3.4 Sample Location with Correction

Sl.No.	Name of the Place
1.	Annamalainagar

Now copy the author/designation name and so on and paste it in the database where it has the exact location. It is better to follow up the same method that may or may not be adopted to the rest of the required bibliographic fields and they are depending on your desk decision. Make your choice to select the required format concerned with the font and other things which have been clearly discussed in latter chapters. You may think about the necessity of this kind of process. As already I have stated this method helps us not only to avoid the typing of the data and also secure uniformity as well as accuracy. The title, author name and other details are sensitive areas where we should not commit even a single mistake as we have to process more number of records that may include more number of authors, co-authors etc. Varieties of bibliographical data should be processed by us within a short duration. The errors which are committed in these areas would also affect the following stages as they have inter-links.

Attention: *However, using the font setup such as caps or small, bold or normal etc., are purely the designer's choice. I didn't force the users of this book to adopt the same font structure discussed above. But, the adopted format would give the neat output as good. Generating all output in caps format is not a usual procedure. As per the requirements the styles such as italics or caps or bold may be applied to the data in order to highlight them.*

3.18 RELATED FILES

Table 3.18.1 List of Files

Sl.No.	Areas
1.	a list of titles
2.	a list of first authors
3.	a list of co-authors
4.	a list of registration
5.	a list for issuing attendance certificates
6.	presentation certificates
7.	participation certificates
8.	a list of themes
9.	a list of addresses
10.	a list of institutions
11.	a conference/seminar volume
12.	an author Index
13.	a subject index
14.	accommodation list
15.	a list of absentees
16.	e-mail addresses

Keep in your mind that committing mistakes in the data even if it is concerned with the first name or surname that might not be a big thing to us but it is a major thing to the concerned authors. Such a thing would be seriously focussed from their desks. In such a case, the person who is behind the process should hold the responsibility and he/she should be in the position of giving a reply reasonably. However, it would not be accepted by the concerned authors and compromising them is quite tough job. Hence I would like to avoid such a perplexing environment and don't like to commit any errors concerned with delegate's details such as their name, title, etc.,

Because once the errors occur in the data entry section, the wrong data would come in all other outputs which have been listed in table 3.18.1. Revising the data without an error in all the areas is supposed to be a possible thing, but it needs more time to accomplish it, which we don't have as we are working for a conference/seminar and not in any other tasks which have a long time to go. Further, whenever you receive the paper/abstract from the delegates desk don't forget to keep the original as it is in a separate folder which is created by you to maintain the original so that the paper could be checked in case of committing errors. If the errors are actually raised from the authors' side that could be captured towards the original file and then the entire responsibility goes to the delegates and it does not face us.

Remember that this type of environment could be faced by us only if we have the original file in our desk. Unless you have the original format, you can never answer their queries that might bring a bad name to your desk. So, always be aware of these kinds of routines and do all the works perfectly even if it is a time consuming process.

Attention: *I don't think that there is an alteration for the said process as I have an experience concerned with errors in titles, authors as discussed above but they have not been raised from my desk and the responsibilities were passed on to the authors desk because they have committed the errors. In some cases i found some errors and they are duly informed to the delegates for correction. For your kind information, I have sat in front of the system for nearly two months and at 6 hours per day during the time of the conference/seminar.*

3.19. THEMES

Once the process of papers is finalized, we could focus

on the themes of the papers that could be done carefully. The received titles would be analyzed by the editors' desk; there the theme could be allotted to the title that would be sent back to our desk for further process. After fixing the theme of the title, the details should be carefully entered into the database where it has the exact location and that could be traced towards the Id of the authors.

Once the theme identifications are finished, all the records could be edited one by one and must be filled with codes which we have opted for the themes. Usually, the codes are in numeric formats that will help to relate the data which has the match. The given screen shot explores the available themes which are created for the event under which the received papers are classified based on the coverage of the area.

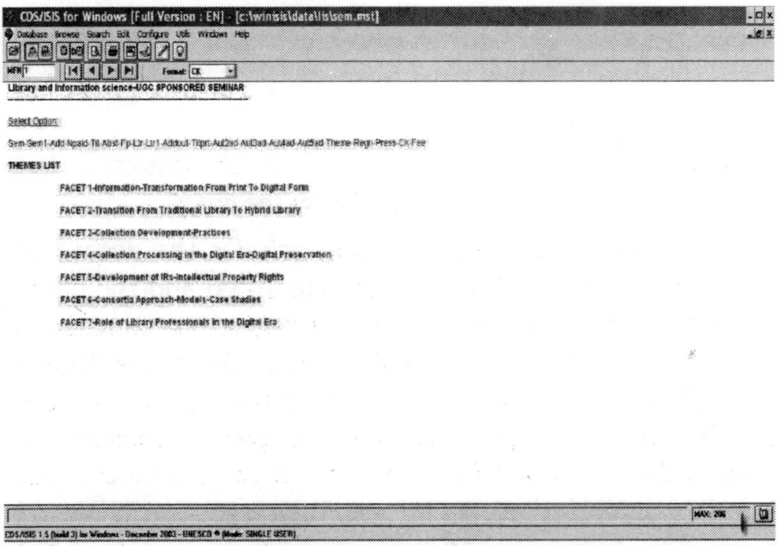

Screen Shot 3.19.1: Themes List

The themes may be generated along with the required details and distributed to the delegates during the time of the event. Nearly seven themes have been structured in which all the received titles are categorized. It is the responsibilities of the editorial board to trace and allot the suitable themes for the received titles. If any paper is found as not related with the theme, the paper may or may not be rejected which also depends on editors' decision. Let us observe the generated screen shot which includes the theme details for id: 100.

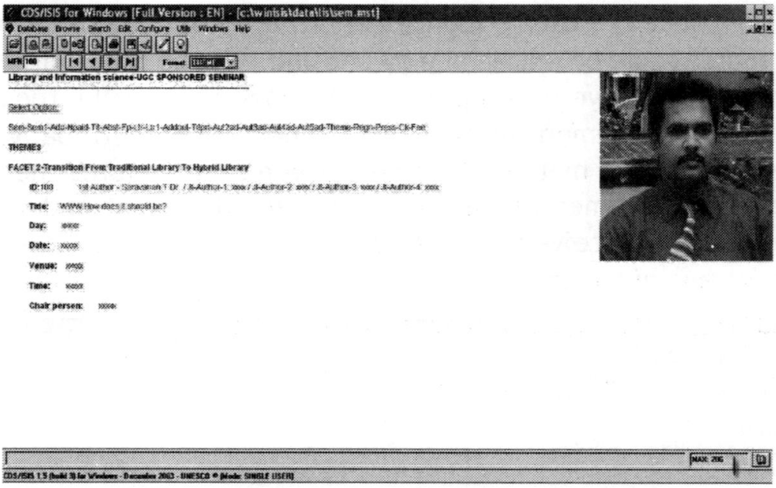

Screen Shot 3.19.2: Theme for the Id:100

The above generated output includes the details of theme in which the title has been classified and the date, day, time, venue, and the chair person for the concerned section also could also be viewed here. The same details would be distributed towards the print format to the delegates so that they could capture the presentation details along with the required information. If you are sure about your data organization only the said theme generation would be possible, otherwise the event routines may suffer. If the provisions are included in your database, you may observe the visual for the chair person of the concerned section; which has not been given here.

***Attention:** After having printed the theme with titles*

list, they must be cross checked by someone else who is working in our team even if they do not possess adequate skills with the system and related works. Because of the general verification, which could be done by the persons as they have to verify the themes, titles, sessions, date, time, venue, chair person, etc., if any, towards the printed versions, so that we could ensure the accuracy of the information; then the list may be distributed to the delegates along with their event kit at the time of the function. While preparing the list of themes do not forget to adopt the indexing system, as it plays a vital role in any kind of data organization and without which our tasks would not be finalized. I have seen many conference/seminar volumes which do not include such an indexing system wherever it is required. This kind of process should not be allowed, as we belong to the Library and Information Science discipline. We can do more than other discipline people as we are the information professionals having more experience and adequate skills in classification and indexing sectors.

Srimurugan, A has pointed out thus *"Don't leave everything to the computer specialists. An equal participation from the Librarians community is a must. Join hands. Pull them into your circle. A coordinated effort shall quench the fire of this illusion of explosion."*

Information management system with technology is a must in the modern scenario. Library and Information Science professionals must have the essential skills not only in their subjects but they are expected to have the adequate potentials in technology too. They can join their hands with the technologically qualified persons as to what Srimurugan, A notes above. Information management system with the help of technology is a cumbersome task. The Library and information science professionals could move along with technologically qualified people to accomplish their task.

However, the preliminary sketches which are concerned with the event should be controlled by us and not by others. When we are responsible to organize some such things, the top slot is ours and the rest of the slots could be occupied by the other professionals when we are sure about our potential in it. Otherwise leave the top slot to the IT qualified people and you can catch the rest of the part. It is a universal truth that in every discipline the professionals who belong to it occupy the predominant place and others are kept behind them. When the event is moving on the track with the assistance of Information Technological tools, the IT qualified people would get much weightage rather than others as they are the experts in that sector. These are the things that should not be happened when Library and Information Science professional organize some events. Why I strongly insist on these things is that the modern users are expecting more kinds of information processing from our desk as we are the authorized people to organize and retrieve any kind of data.

3.20. PRESENTATION LIST

This section discusses the preparation of a final list for presentations that include the details of the authors who are permitted to deliver their papers during the event. As already have been discussed in this book regarding the preparation of volume, it includes the abstracts/full texts that have some restrictions regarding the registration related matters. There may or may not be a chance to face the environment as some of the delegates who have done their registration on the spot may have an interest to present the papers even if it is not covered by the volume *(Note that these are purely local variations that depend on your authorities' desk and I got time to face these kind of situations so that the points have been revised here)*. In this case, the delegates might be taken to the authorities' desk for further processing, as we are not the decision makers here. Let these kinds of routines come to the authorities' desk. For some of the authors, we might not receive the fee, but the paper that exists may include single or multiple authors. Remember the rule that when no one is registered, the paper would be excluded from the volume which I have already discussed clearly in the previous sections. Now the question is whether the paper would be considered for presentation or not. The decision could be taken by the authorities. But, the database will not include these papers in the presentation list as well as in the volume for the persons who have not registered, because of the predefined rules. These kinds of local variations would definitely violate data organization. Now, the command flows from the authorities' desk to consider the said paper. What could we do?. There would be no more time to carry out this task through the database and I opted for some alternatives that also have been discussed in the previous sections. Remember when we have the said alternative process; the indexing process would suffer as the database will generate the index for the data which are covered by the database only. The classified systems also could not consider the data which exist outside the boundaries of the database. Because when we have some data in other files that would not help us to organize them effectively as to what kind of output we would like to generate. I faced this kind of environment by the given way that first I generated the presentation list based on the classified indexing system. Then they are exported to the spreadsheet editors using the standard format, where I clubbed the excluded items dynamically which are available in some other files and then the final report is generated.

Attention: *Though it is an easy way to export the data from one package to other, chances are there to violate the accuracy and standardization, if we could not take care of it. The delimiters which are used by us to split the data should be the same as one with what we have adopted in the database.*

Observe the given screen shot which explores the data export towards the text mode from one place to another place.

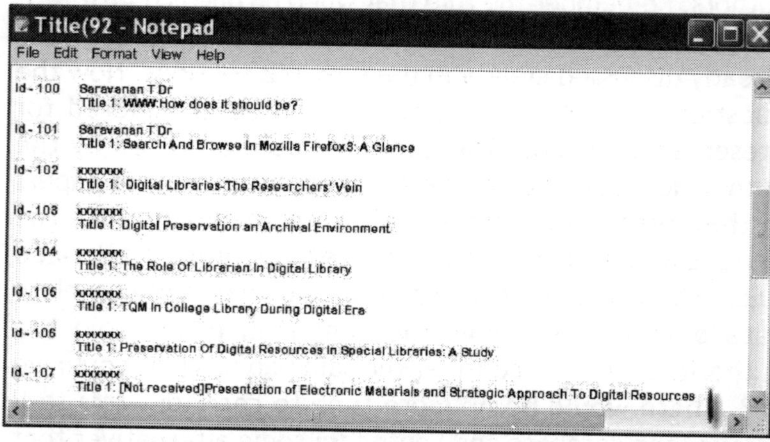

Title(92 - Notepad

File Edit Format View Help

Id-100 Saravanan T Dr
Title 1: WWW:How does it should be?

Id-101 Saravanan T Dr
Title 1: Search And Browse In Mozilla Firefox3: A Glance

Id-102 xxxxxxx
Title 1: Digital Libraries-The Researchers' Vein

Id-103 xxxxxxx
Title 1: Digital Preservation an Archival Environment

Id-104 xxxxxxx
Title 1: The Role Of Librarian In Digital Library

Id-105 xxxxxxx
Title 1: TQM In College Library During Digital Era

Id-106 xxxxxxx
Title 1: Preservation Of Digital Resources In Special Libraries: A Study

Id-107 xxxxxxx
Title 1: [Not received]Presentation of Electronic Materials and Strategic Approach To Digital Resources

Screen Shot 3.20.1: Presentation List-Exported Textual mode

In the above screen shot, the data has been generated by their ID sequence and converted into the text format because of the violations which we have in the previous sections. The same format has been taken towards the document mode also that could be viewed from the given screen shot.

The following screen shot lets you to observe the records which do not receive the full text and has to the abstract only till the beginning of the event. But, the authors for the mentioned papers have registered properly and some unforeseen reasons might be behind the delay of the paper. In such a case, the abstract would be included in the volume as we do not receive the concerned paper from the authors' desk even though proper communications are sent by us to their desk. But they may come for the presentation on the scheduled date as they have the rights by the way of registration. Hence, the presentation list should include their details with the identification 'Not received' which is noted to us about its current status.

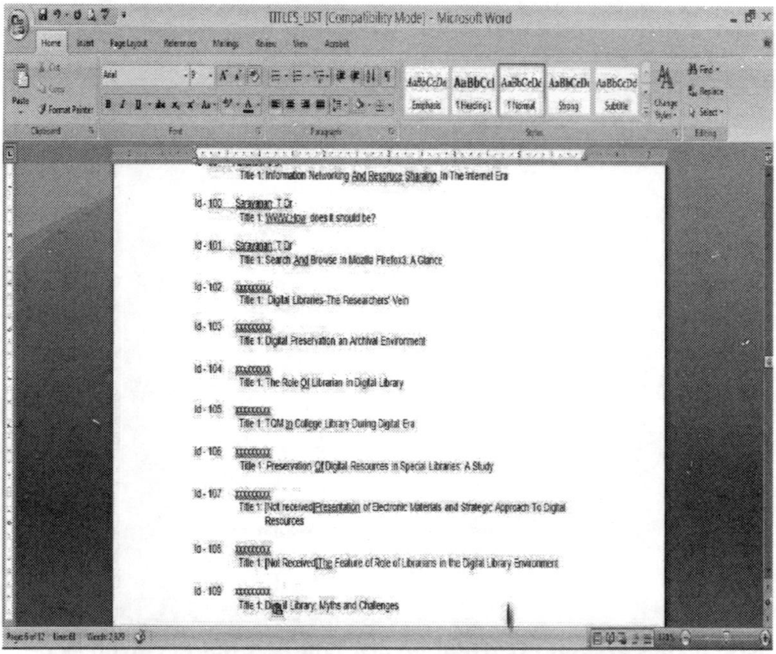

Screen Shot 3.20.2: Presentation List-Exported Document mode

The above outputs have been generated according to the indexing system in which the delegates' ID has been opted for the Indexing purpose. The output includes the ID, Name of the Author(s), and Title of the Paper. Let us observe the following output which has been generated towards the spreadsheet tool.

The above screen shot includes the Theme and Title followed by the author's name. All the themes have been indexed in which the title and an author(s) name have been classified.

In the above screen shot, one could observe the indexing system which I have acquired to generate the output to prepare the list. All the themes are indexed under the facet name in which the authors have been classified,

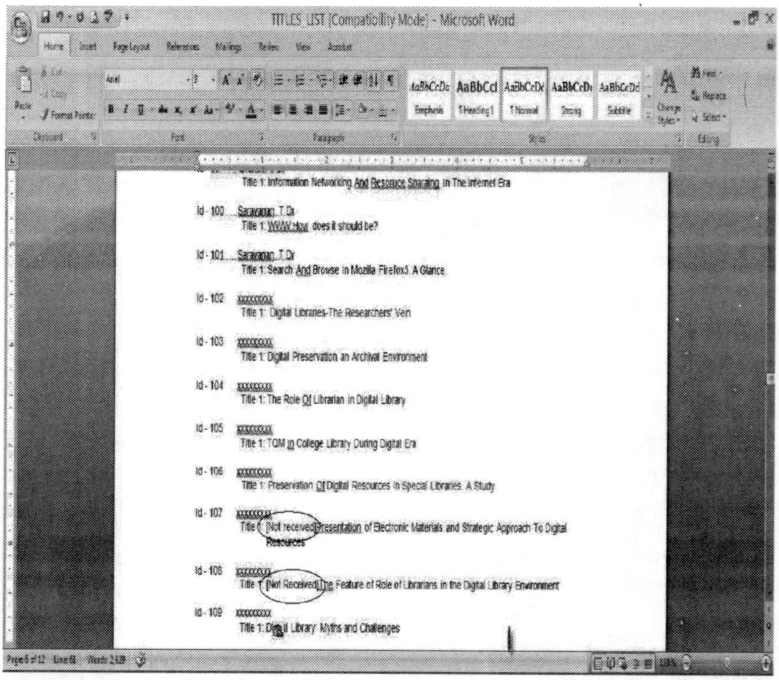

Screen Shot 3.20.3: Presentation List-Full Text Not Received Mode

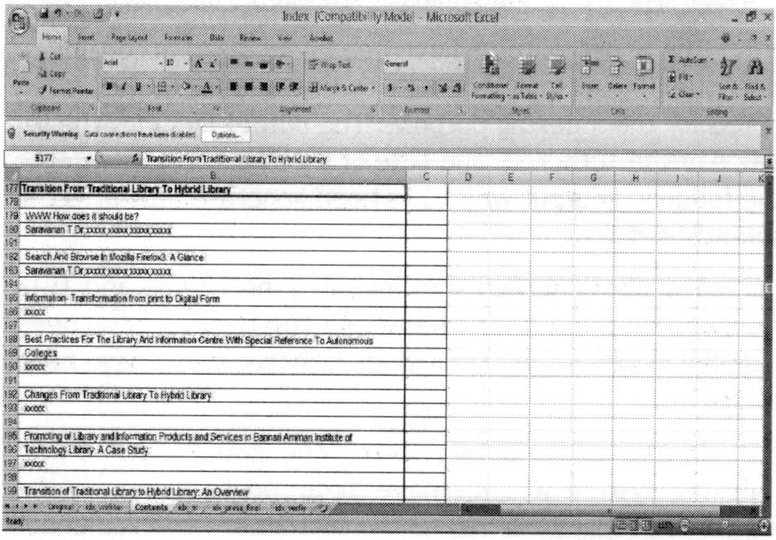

Screen Shot 3.20.4: Presentation List-Spreadsheet Mode

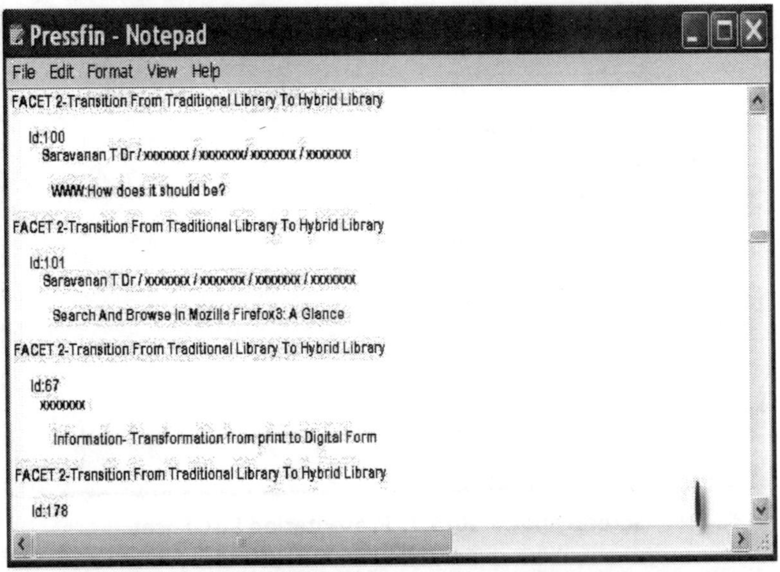

Screen Shot 3.20.5: Presentation List-Classified indexing system

followed by the title that could be possible in the WinISIS® application package, as it is one of the advantages of the package. Such a complicated process could be easily handled with the said application.

Let us go through the given screen shot that clearly indicates the order of the data as to how they have been classified. You could observe that the facets which have the same name, have the sequence in which the authors have come according to the ascending order whereas the Ids are scattered as it is the concept of classified indexing system, where the related terms would be grouped together. It is quite natural for getting different Ids when we group the terms under one key term as all the related term may or may not exist in various Ids.

The given screen shot shows the output according to the sequence of ID which has been arranged under the facets.

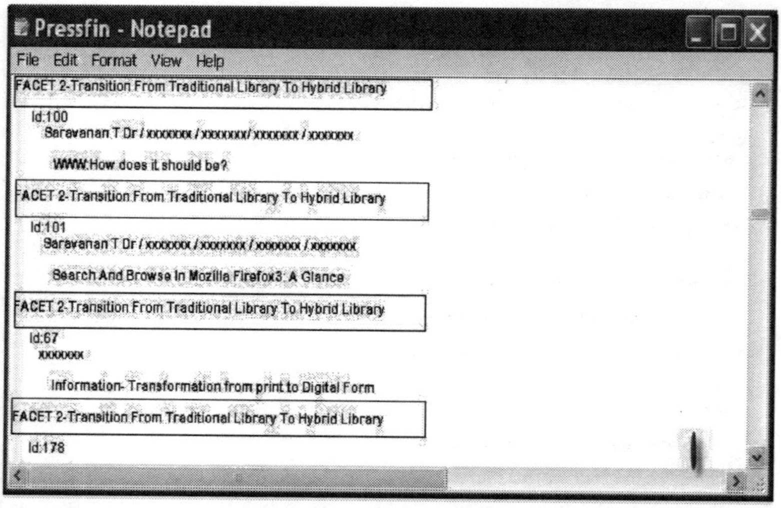

Screen Shot 3.20.5.1: Presentation List-Facet wise classified indexing system

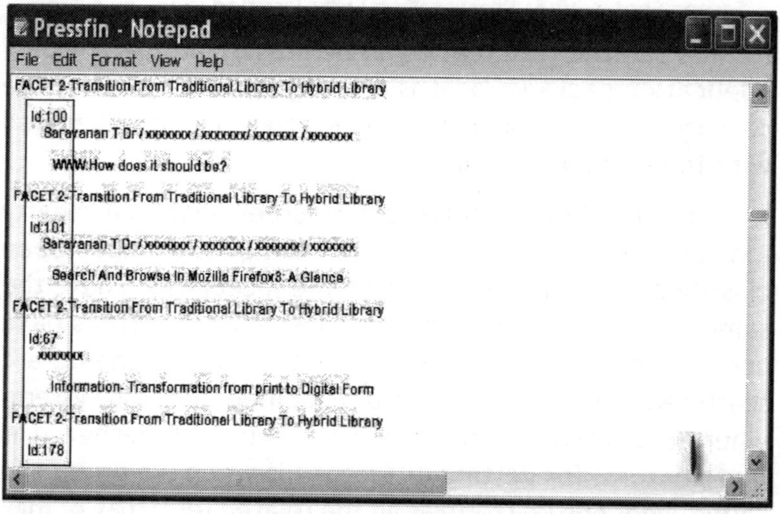

Screen Shot 3.20.5.2: Presentation List-ID wise classified indexing system

When you observe the above two screen shots, the indexing system could be easily observed.

Attention: *It is a must to take care while generating* *these kinds of outputs as there may be a chance to commit the errors in the programme sectors that would lead in the result of wrong match. Probabilities for the errors are;*

1. *Mismatch between the facet and an Id.*
2. *Mismatch between the facet and the delegate's name.*
3. *Mismatch between the facet and the title.*
4. *Mismatch between the Id and the delegate's name.*
5. *Mismatch between the Id and the title.*

If one line would skip from the exact location the entire output would be collapsed as we are not handling the records of 1 or 2 but may include more number of records which could not be handled manually. The given screen shot clearly indicates the maximum record length after having the data conversion.

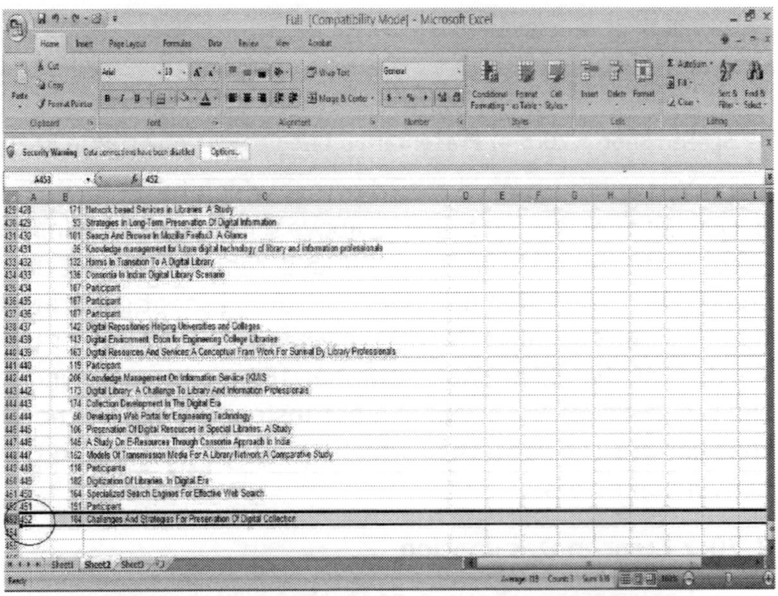

Screen Shot 3.20.5.3: Presentation List-Total Record Status

Let us observe the following screen shots that explore

the errors which could have occurred while exporting the data.

3.20.1. Error in ID

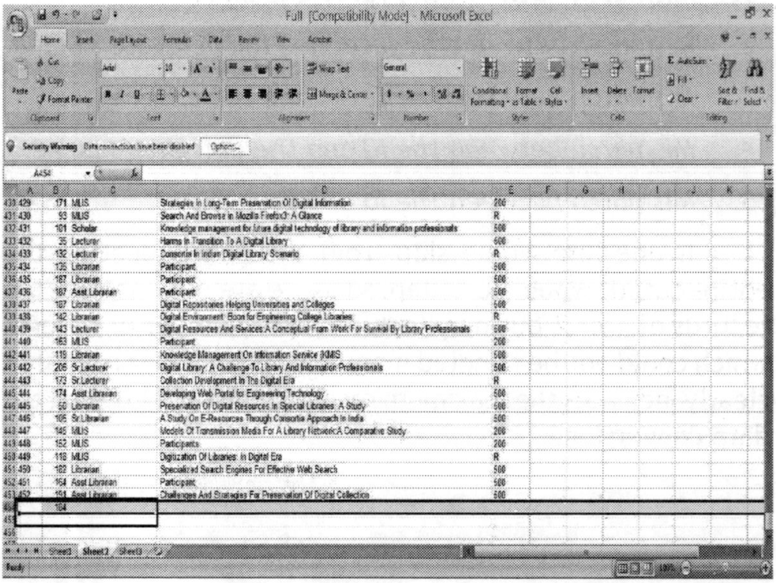

Screen Shot 3.20.5.4: Presentation List-Conversion Error in ID

You could observe the Id errors which have occurred during data conversion from the above screen shot. Maximum records are traced from the previous screen shot as 452 that come under the serial number. The spread sheet generated number is 453 because the first row has been allotted for the headers of the data. The ID number 184 might come under the range 452 of the serial number instead of that of the ID that has got the range 454 which could happen due to the conversion errors.

3.20.2 Error in Designation

Look at the above screen shot which explores the entire data along with the errors in the designation field. The ID 191,184 actually has the designations as Asst.Librarian but the data which we look here do not give that due to the conversion errors. Hence, they have been misplaced and yields the results 191 belongs to the designation 'Librarian' and this is the major data violation that would affect all other routines of the data processing which have been briefly discussed in the previous sections.

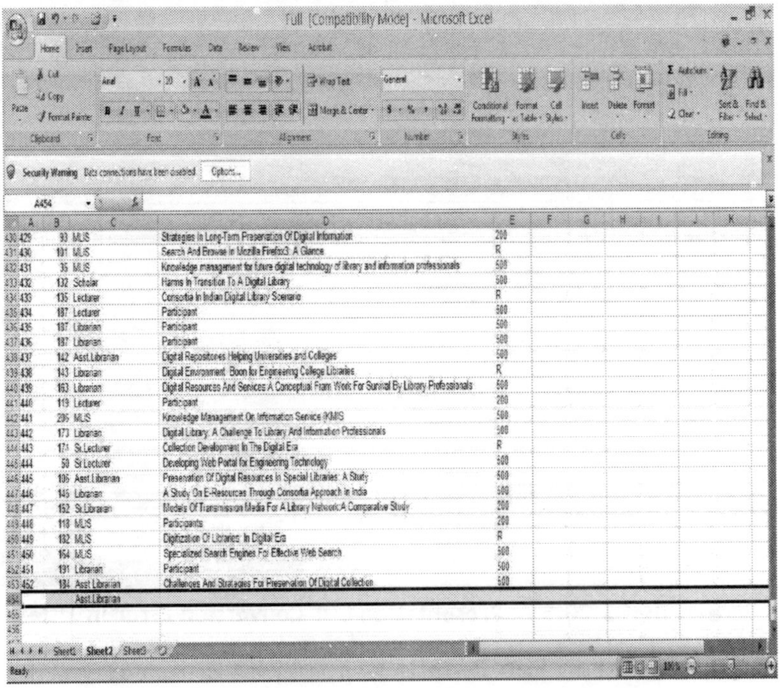

Screen Shot 3.20.5.5: Presentation List-Conversion Error in Designation

3.20.3. Error in Titles

The above screen shot gives the wrong data conversion which could occur in the title field when the data are transferred from the database to spread sheet option. The author whose Id is 191 is identified as participant of the event and the said author has no connection with the presentation. Because of the errors which we have seen above the identification 'Participant' has been skipped to the next record under Id 184 and the title which is related to Id 184 has also got skipped to the next level.

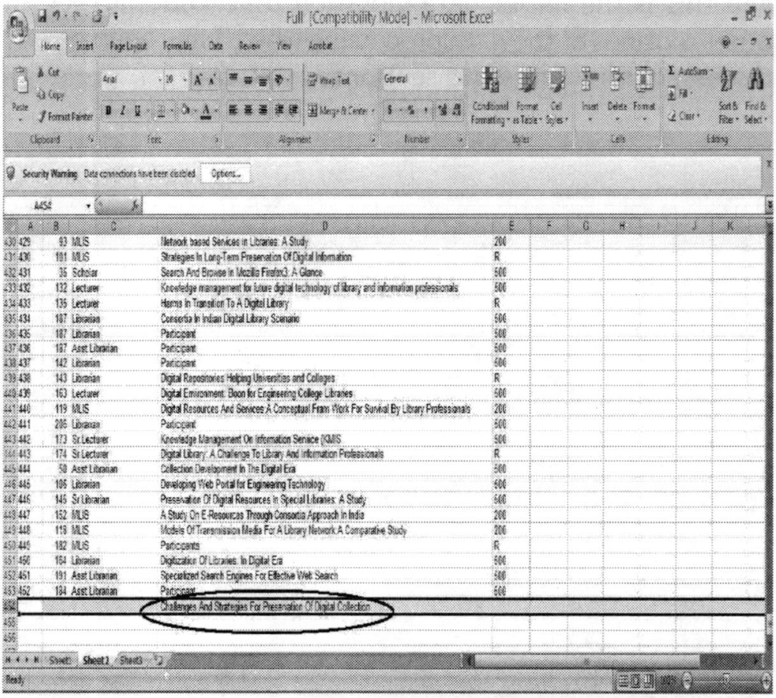

Screen Shot 3.20.5.6: Presentation List-Conversion Error in Titles

3.20.4. Error in Fee Details

When we do not take enough attention in data conversion area, the errors would occur in the fee section also. The last record has no data except the fee Rs.500 which might be in the row 453 which has the serial number 452 and Id 184. The caps form 'R' denotes reference that indicates that the author has registered already that could be located from some other previous Ids in which the author has come as first or co-author. The code 'R' has been adopted by me to identify these kinds of data towards the program and the details have been clearly explained along with the visual identification in the previous sections. From the figure it is realized that the Ids of those having the codes 'R' are skipped and thereby cause data violation.

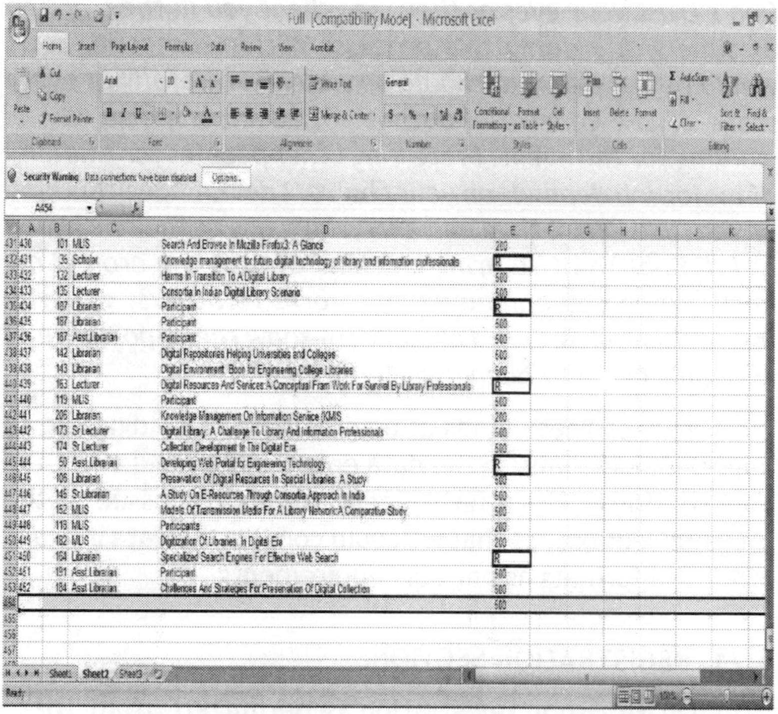

	A	B	C	D	E
431	430	101	MLIS	Search And Browse In Mozilla Firefox3: A Glance	200
432	431	35	Scholar	Knowledge management for future digital technology of library and information professionals	R
433	432	132	Lecturer	Harms In Transition To A Digital Library	500
434	433	135	Lecturer	Consortia In Indian Digital Library Scenario	500
435	434	187	Librarian	Participant	R
436	435	187	Librarian	Participant	500
437	436	187	Asst.Librarian	Participant	500
438	437	142	Librarian	Digital Repositories Helping Universities and Colleges	500
439	438	143	Librarian	Digital Environment Boon for Engineering College Libraries	500
440	439	163	Lecturer	Digital Resources And Services A Conceptual Fram Work For Survival By Library Professionals	R
441	440	119	MLIS	Participant	500
442	441	206	Librarian	Knowledge Management On Information Service (KMIS	200
443	442	173	Sr Lecturer	Digital Library: A Challenge To Library And Information Professionals	500
444	443	174	Sr Lecturer	Collection Development In The Digital Era	500
445	444	50	Asst.Librarian	Developing Web Portal for Engineering Technology	R
446	445	106	Librarian	Preservation Of Digital Resources In Special Libraries: A Study	500
447	446	145	Sr Librarian	A Study On E-Resources Through Consortia Approach In India	500
448	447	152	MLIS	Models Of Transmission Media For A Library Network:A Comparative Study	500
449	448	119	MLIS	Participants	200
450	449	182	MLIS	Digitization Of Libraries In Digital Era	200
451	450	164	Librarian	Specialized Search Engines For Effective Web Search	R
452	451	191	Asst.Librarian	Participant	500
453	452	184	Asst Librarian	Challenges And Strategies For Preservation Of Digital Collection	500
454					500

Screen Shot 3.20.5.7: Presentation List-Conversion Error in Fee details

Attention: *The screen shots concerned with data conversion errors, which are given above show data arrangement according to the sequence of the authors, and hence the Ids and other related data have been scattered. If the records are in limited range the problems could be rectified. When we organize more number of data it is not possible to locate the errors where they have occurred. Conferences and Seminars are such a big event that could need more attention while handling the data with the help of technology for the sorting purposes. This is supposed to* *be a critical situation and hence unless you are familiar with these things, don't attempt this process as you are responsible for everything whatever that would happen. Don't trust your eyes as they may cheat you in the fraction of time while doing this process. Within a second, rows would be skipped that should be watched carefully at every stage of the generated output with someone else who is working for the event. Preferring other peoples for this kind of major job depends on your choice. I do not have this kind of verification method and everything has been done by me as I did not want to bring any kind of problem around my desk. When you hand over the works to others, give the instructions clearly and make them know the importance of the job which has been assigned to them.*

To face these kinds of environment it is advisable to maintain uniformity in the data entry section and avoid the punctuations, which have been already discussed in the previous sections, so that we could convert the data into any other file formats as per our requirements.

3.21. REGISTRATION SECTIONS

On the spot registration is permitted in all these events. At the beginning of the first day of the programme, there may be a chance to face too much crowd which includes both the registered as well as unregistered delegates. Hence, it is better to open three counters to face the delegates and also that would be helpful to carry out our routines without any burdens. The first counter could be opened for persons who have come for registration. The second one could be allotted to receive the persons who have already registered. The third one could be opened to issue the kit which has the entire details of the conference/ seminar. Some of the routines are essential in all the counters as they have to verify the author's details with the existing database. The complete verification should be done before handing over the kit to the delegates by way of checking their ID and other related things, which have been issued by the counters first and second.

Here it is an important task to keep the necessity of the verification of the ID in our mind as it plays the vital role up to the end of the event and acts as a backbone of the database. *(Here the term 'ID' denotes the unique number which is allotted by us to the delegates towards the database)* Let us see the routines of the three said counters one by one for better understanding.

3.21.1. Routines of the First counter

Attention: *All three counters should be equipped with systems and other infrastructures. The person who is responsible for the said places should have adequate skills in technology sector so that they could carry out the tasks. We can provide more supporting person who could assist the delegates in front of the counters to follow up the rules and regulations. Offering more system facilities and man power are all local variations that depend on your surroundings.*

Assume that the first counter has been allotted exclusively for the purpose of spot registration where the delegates could come and register on the day of the event. The delegates who have already registered need not approach the first counter for any purpose. Hence proper guidelines/displays could be provided near the counters from which the delegates would move on the right track. Remember that the database created is being utilized in all the three counters. *(I have adopted the single user mode only due to our local variations and the networking concept may be adopted for more performances rather than the single mode.)*

In this counter, the person who wants to register has

to tell the ID, in case if they have already received the communication from our desk. Keep it in your mind once the communication is dispatched from our desk to the delegates, it is assumed that the unique ID also has been given to the concerned author(s). Here the thing is they have not registered till the beginning of the conference; hence they have approached the first counter. If the ID exists in the database, confirm the author's name and other details *(here the visual option enables us to confirm the identity)*, then collect the exact fee that could be entered into the database immediately. Already we have all the bibliographical data for the author(s) in the database, if the author(s) already having the ID only. In such a case edit the concerned record towards the ID which is given by the author(s) and feed the fee related details such as amount, bank/cash, receipt numbers etc. Remember that there are only two options in the registration part, they are

1. Already paid
2. On the spot registration.

We must be careful to enter these data as we already have data in registration area for many authors as they may or may not be the first or co-authors. Observe the given examples.

For instance the ID:100 includes five authors. Of the five, the first three authors might have registered already and the rest two authors may have opted for the on the spot registration. The record would be edited by the ID:100 and the fourth or fifth author location should be carefully identified for the data entry. Because all the five authors fall under the same title, they have got the ID:100. So whenever we open the record by the ID:100 it would show the five authors along with the required bibliographical details. Hence, it is possible to easily trace the author(s) who have come for spot registration as their data have been arranged separately, which would enable the in- charge of the counter to enter the data accurately into the database.

If the author(s) is a new one and does not have the ID already he/she must get a new ID from our desk. If enough time is there, the data about the author(s) could be entered directly into the database or else issue a printed registration form to them to get the required details. Collect the fee and verify the required bibliographic details such as name, designation, etc., which should be taken with care as the data have not yet been fed into the database. When time comes, the data which are available in the receipt could be entered into the database and the time taken should not exceed beyond a day. Within the schedule of the event, the complete bibliographic details should be prepared with the help of the database so that we could prepare all records as per the requirements. Remember that the registration form would be issued to authors who do not have the unique ID. The collected filled in registration forms should be preserved in separate files as they might be the evidence for any future reference related to the author or fee or anything concerned. For future reference, these kinds of maintenance are a must as data storage in electronic format may or may not be trust worthy in the long run because of its demerit. Having manual records always help us to secure the data even when they brings more works to our desk.

The given screen shot enables you to capture the sample registration format which could be adopted to maintain fee and other bibliographic details of the authors in the first counter. Provisions are there to collect the author visual as our database has the future to access the bibliographic details of any author along with their visuals. Hence, it is the duty of the first counter in charge to collect the visual copy which might be in electronic format which would be linked to the database after having been fed the required bibliographic details into the structured database.

Attention: *The visuals of the authors are supposed to be in our desk when they send the paper to an event so that we could carry out our task. But in the case of authors who have come for spot registration, the visual might be collected and processed without any delay.*

ANNAMALAI UNIVERSITY

DEPARTMENT OF LIBRARY AND INFORMATION SCIENCE

REGISTRATION FORM

Sl.Number:________ DATE :____________

ID :____________

Fix Visual here

NAME :________________________

SEX : Male / Female

DESIGNATION :________________________

DEPARTMENT :________________________

INSTITUTION :________________________

ADDRESS :________________________

____

Mobile :________________________

E-mail :________________________

Paper Title (if any): ____

____

FEE:

Amount: ____________ Balance (If any)____________

Accommodation: Yes / No

____

Received By __________________ (Signature of the Counter In charge)

1. Certificate – Yes / No 2. Attendance – Yes/No

Screen Shot 3.21.1.1: Sample Registration Format

3.21.1.1. Generating Receipt

Though many facilities are available in the database to take the report in the said format there is a need to maintain the manual receipt as its requirements have been discussed in the previous sections. You could generate the receipt from the database after having entered the bibliographic details into the database and then the generated receipt must be handed over to the concerned author before he leaves the institution where the event has been scheduled. You could observe the sample generated receipt towards the database from the given screen shot where the author visual also has been visualized for the exact identification. This is the sample receipt output for the first author with the ID:100. If any co-author(s) exist the same receipt output would be made possible. This feature enables us to take the immediate output while dealing routines at the spot registration counters.

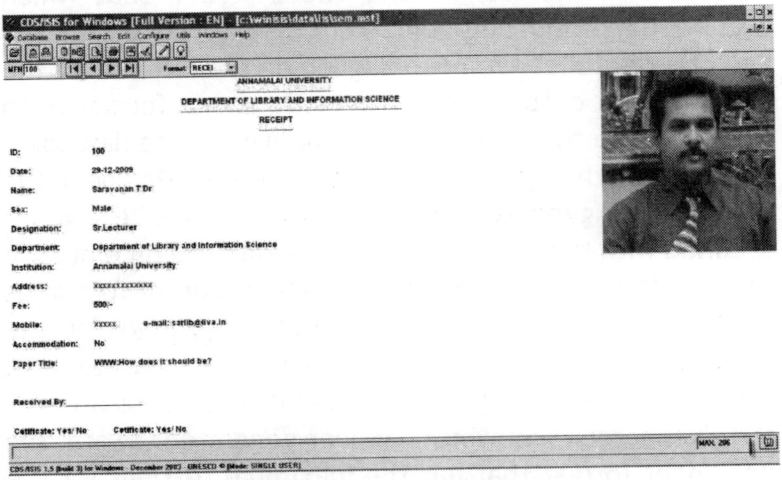

Screen Shot 3.21.1.2: Sample Receipt

The receipt report has been explored by the given screen shots that show the text format as well as document format, as the package offers multiple features to generate any kind of output as per our requirements

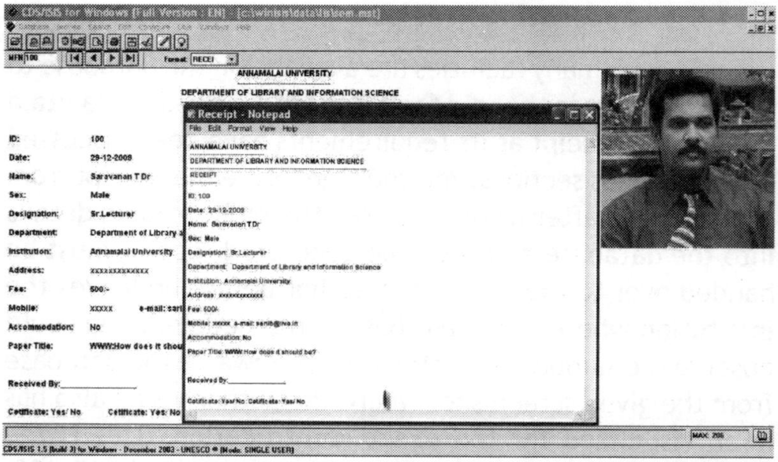

Screen Shot 3.21.1.3: Sample Receipt-.Txt output

As you might be familiar with the text editing tools that text output format has less features, it will not permit us to take the output as to what we have generated in the database. Please look at the above screen shot which explores the receipt output in .txt mode in which the headers and other details have been aligned on the left side of the file. The text output may not give the exact format as to what we have the as structure of the data in the database. Generally all the data will be arranged on the left side of the file when we generate the report in text mode. If you are satisfied with this output you can generate the receipt as in the said format. If you prefer the receipt output format as in the database output format better you go for the document format output that gives all the features to reset the imported item as per our expectations. Let us observe the given screen shot which has been generated towards the document format that has the maximum settings for the exported data as to what we have been expecting to generate actually. However, we have to carry out some alignments which are less compared with the text format output.

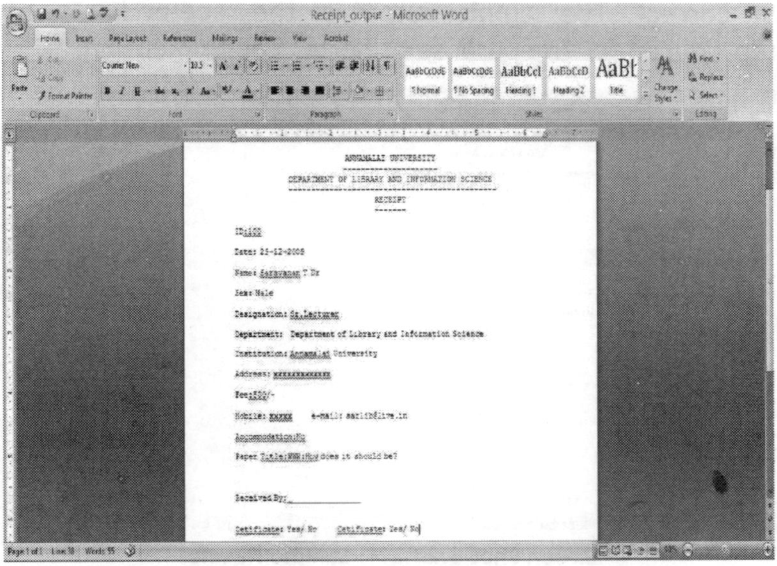

Screen Shot 3.21.1.4: Sample Receipt-.Doc output

Attention: *But remember that we are not in a position to use any kind of text editing packages for data conversion process as the seminar/conference would be commenced soon and we have no time to process the output in the said formats. Hence, the receipt could be taken from the database directly with the same format as the package gives multiple features to generate any form of report. So, in the peak hours better not to go for any other package for receipt output. The purpose for which, the said outputs have been generated is to realize the power of the WinISIS® only.*

3.21.2. Routines of the Second Counter

This section has been formulated exclusively for persons, who have already registered. That means they must have a unique ID, which has been offered by us. So, it is the duty of the in charge of this section to make the cross verification with the ID, which is expressed by the author and then generate the receipt if the identifications are found to be correct. The sample output of the receipt has been reproduced for the purpose of better comprehension.

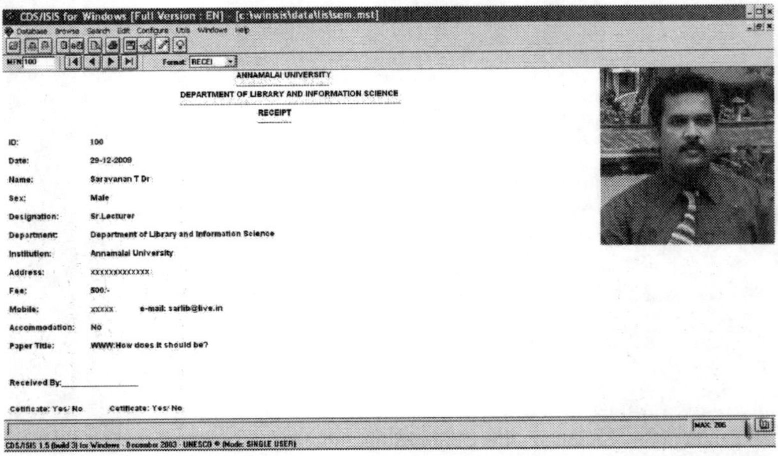

Screen Shot 3.21.2.1: Sample Receipt

Attention: *Don't forget to get the signature from the delegates against their names which are available in the printed full format output that includes all the bibliographic details of the authors. After getting the signature only, you should issue the receipt and let them to move on to the third counter. The supporting staff members may help to carry out this kind of work as one person alone could never do these kinds of jobs. Further, there may be a chance to face more crowds during the seminar/conference time. Hence to organize the registration sections properly without facing any difficulties there is a need to depute more manpower as this section deals with the financial matter. Remember that manpower with the technology skills are added advantages to this section.*

After having cleared the routines with this section, let the delegates move to the third one, where they could collect the necessary kit related to the program as per the routines which have been discussed already.

Observe the given screen shot which gives the major bibliographic details of the author(s) and this format could be utilized in the registration counters where we need to verify the data and get the signatures of the authors.

The first column of the given screen shot is concerned with the sl.no., followed by name of the author, unique id, designation, institution, title of the paper, fee and the last one is exclusively for the purpose of getting his/her signature. I have hidden all other authors name and their institutions as these things are concerned with the copy rights that have been already discussed in the previous sections. So, whenever we issue the receipt to the author they must put their signature against their name as shown below. The following output should be in the printed form and must be in all the counters of the registration section so that any details could be captured as and when required.

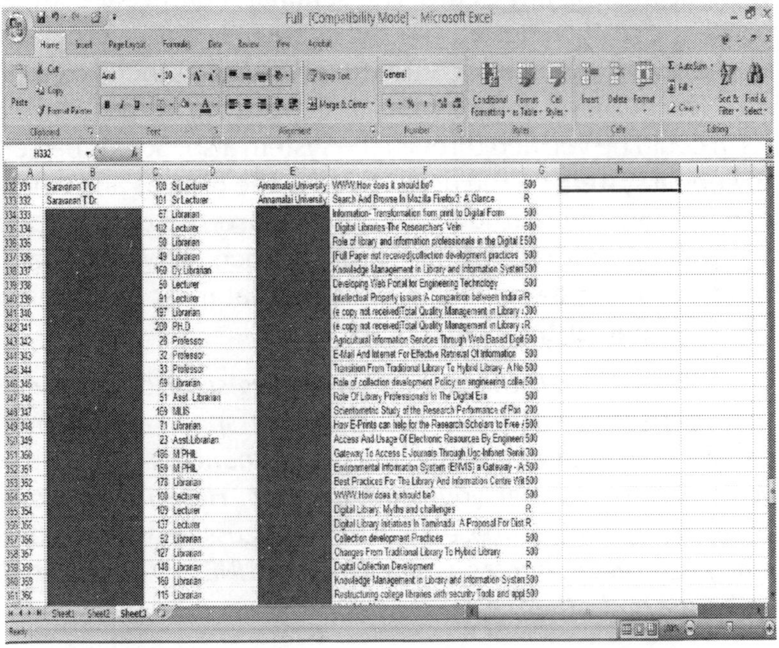

	A	B	C	D	E	F	G	H
332	331	Saravanan T Dr	100	Sr Lecturer	Annamalai University	WWW How does it should be?	500	
333	332	Saravanan T Dr	101	Sr Lecturer	Annamalai University	Search And Browse In Mozilla Firefox3: A Glance	R	
334	333		67	Librarian		Information- Transformation from print to Digital Form	500	
335	334		102	Lecturer		Digital Libraries-The Researchers' Vein	500	
336	335		98	Librarian		Role of library and information professionals in the Digital E	500	
337	336		49	Librarian		[Full Paper not received]collection development practices	500	
338	337		160	Dy Librarian		Knowledge Management in Library and information System	500	
339	338		50	Lecturer		Developing Web Portal for Engineering Technology	500	
340	339		91	Lecturer		Intellectual Property issues A comparison between India a	R	
341	340		197	Librarian		(e copy not received)Total Quality Management in Library	300	
342	341		200	PH.D		(e copy not received)Total Quality Management in Library	R	
343	342		28	Professor		Agricultural Information Services Through Web Based Digi	500	
344	343		32	Professor		E-Mail And Internet For Effective Retrieval Of Information	500	
345	344		33	Professor		Transition From Traditional Library To Hybrid Library- A Ne	500	
346	345		69	Librarian		Role of collection development Policy on engineering colle	500	
347	346		51	Asst. Librarian		Role Of Library Professionals In The Digital Era	500	
348	347		169	MLIS		Scientometric Study of the Research Performance of Pon	200	
349	348		71	Librarian		How E-Prints can help for the Research Scholars to Free	500	
350	349		23	Asst.Librarian		Access And Usage Of Electronic Resources By Engineeri	500	
351	350		186	M PHIL		Gateway To Access E-Journals Through Ugc-Infonet Seri	300	
352	351		159	M PHIL		Environmental Information System (ENVIS) a Gateway - A	500	
353	352		178	Librarian		Best Practices For The Library And Information Centre Wit	500	
354	353		100	Lecturer		WWW How does it should be?	500	
355	354		109	Lecturer		Digital Library: Myths and challenges	R	
356	355		137	Lecturer		Digital Library Initiatives In Tamilnadu A Proposal For Dist	R	
357	356		52	Librarian		Collection development Practices	500	
358	357		127	Librarian		Changes From Traditional Library To Hybrid Library	500	
359	358		148	Librarian		Digital Collection Development	R	
360	359		160	Librarian		Knowledge Management in Library and information System	500	
361	360		115	Librarian		Restructuring college libraries with security Tools and appl	500	

Screen Shot 3.21.2.2: Format to get the signature of the author

Tracing the authors towards the said output is an easy job as the file has been indexed on the basis of the authors' name. Hence all the authors would be arranged in an ascending order with the required bibliographical details and make our search easy and so compact.

Attention: *While indexing the data be sure about the related bibliographic details as there may be a chance to get the misplacement of the data that will violate the entire process.*

3.21.3. Routines of the Third Counter

This counter is fully responsible for all the things which are concerned with the seminar/conference. It is the duty of the counter in charge that they have to verify the receipt/ payment details, which have been produced by the authors so that the section in-charge could issue the kit to them without making any delay. The seminar/conference kit is nothing that includes all the things such as entire program of the event, seminar/conference volume, lunch tokens, etc. The authors' details which are available in the printed form could be verified through the system also. So it is better to keep a system on the desk to verify the data as and when needed. But the authors who have registered on the spot could show their receipt for the verification, only if the data were not yet updated in the database that must be done by the in charge of the first counter.

Attention: *If the systems in the registration counters are connected with the network, the spot registration details also could be viewed in other counters. Structure your database as per your environment. Here no network concepts of the database have been discussed as there are many reference sources available in the UNESCO authorized webpage and other related sites.*

3.21.4. Routines to issue the Seminar/Conference Certificates

One of the major tasks of the seminar/conference is to prepare the certificates as it requires more attention to prepare the list of the authors and writing/printing their name and other details on the certificates. While preparing the list, it is an important thing to verify the presence of the authors in the seminar/conference. Generally, the certificates are to be issued to the authors who have showed their presence in the event and should not be issued to persons who have not attended as it may cause a lot of problems anywhere at any time. So, it is advisable not to issue the certificates to the persons who are not in the event as on date. Observe the following seven criteria from the given table that enables you to capture the data that who would be eligible and not eligible to receive the seminar/ conference certificates.

Table 3.21.4.1 Authors' Eligibility Criteria to Receive the Certificates

Sl.No.	Status of the Author(s)	Eligible	Not eligible
1.	Not Registered		✓
2.	Registered and attended	✓	
3.	Registered and not attended		✓
4.	Attended without Registration		✓
5.	Spot Registered and attended	✓	
6.	Spot Registered and not attended		✓

The report for preparing the certificates could be generated from the database after having finalized the data entry which includes the spot registration details also. The new ID details must be fed into the database on the day itself so that we can generate the reports for the entire data.

The structured database will generate the report that includes the details of the author, title, fee and other details for preparing the certificates. The database would not generate the report for the authors who have not registered and attended the seminar/conference. So, verifying these two conditions is a must before processing the certificates. Database contains data. It is the duty of the database developer to extract the required data as it is not the right process to generate the report for all the authors who have registered and not registered/ attended and not attended.

Let us capture the fee details of the authors from the given screen shot which has been reproduced here for better understanding before processing the certificates to the authors.

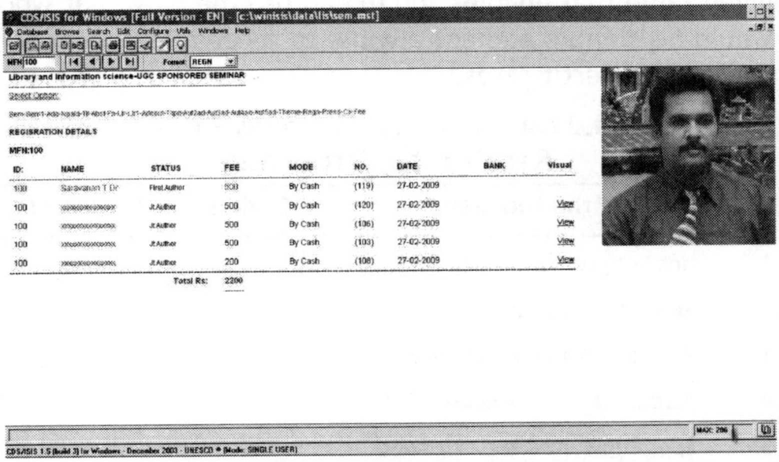

Screen Shot 3.21.4.2 List of authors with fee details

After completing the spot registration process, I have generated three types of output for the purpose of preparing the list of authors who are eligible to receive the certificates. The three types of outputs are categorized as Staff, Scholars and Students. Thus the generated output could be observed from the given screen shots. This type of classification of authors would make our work easier and also keep us from unnecessary confusions such as duplication of authors, titles, etc which have been clearly discussed in the previous sections. Further, categorization of authors would help us to handover the works which are related to the certificates preparation. In case we prefer the handwritten format it is better to write the name of the author, title and other details on the certificates. To carry out these jobs, we need three teams and they would take care of the three categories of authors. Let the first team for prepare the certificates for the Staff members, the second team for Scholars and the third team may take the job for student categories. Don't forget that whatever be the team we have for these processes the complete list of authors for whom the certificates are to be prepared should be on their desk to have a verification as and when required and without the list the preparations of the certificates may cause many kinds of problems that may be related with the data such as

1. Author initial
2. Name
3. Institution
4. Place
5. Title
6. Designation, etc.

The given screen shot shows the generated list of output for the Staff members.

The person who is in the process of preparing certificates can get enough details from the generated output. But he/she must have the alertness to pick up the required data from the output as the data are not in limited numbers.

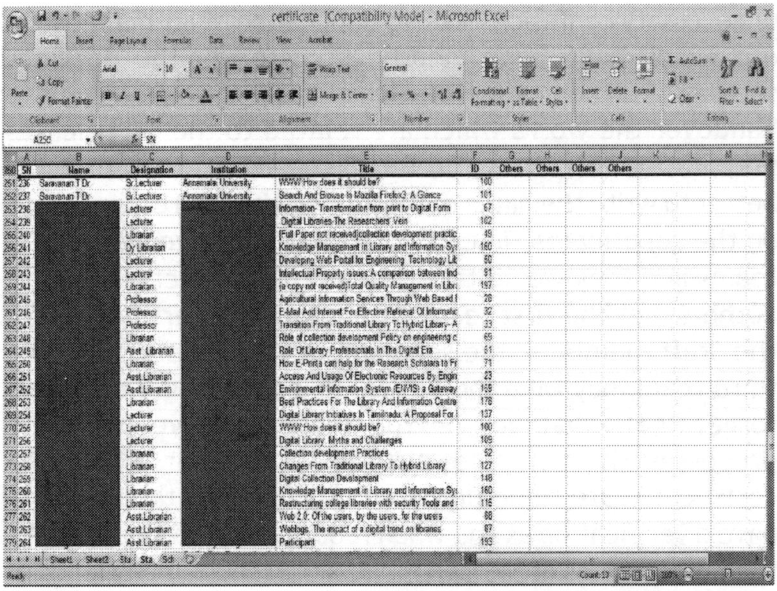

Screen Shot 3.21.4.3 Certificates-List of authors (Staff)

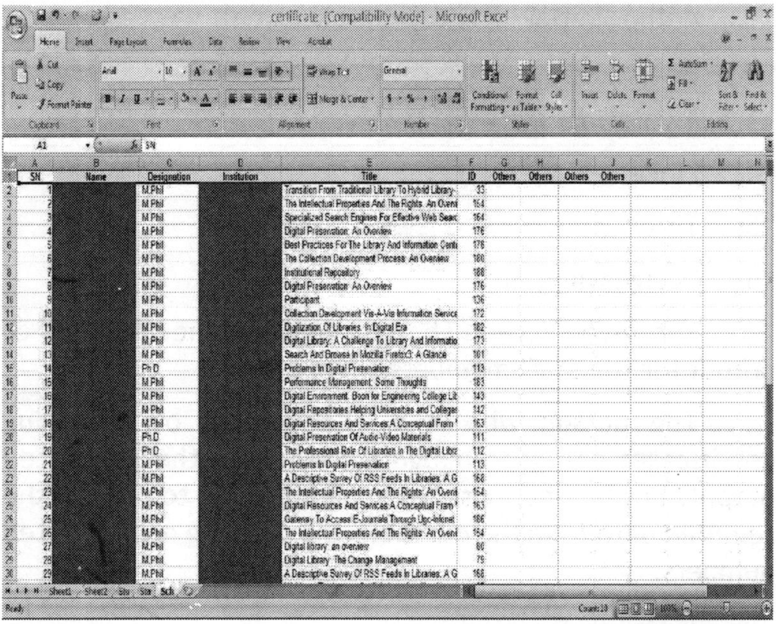

Screen Shot 3.21.4.4 Certificates-List of authors (Scholars)

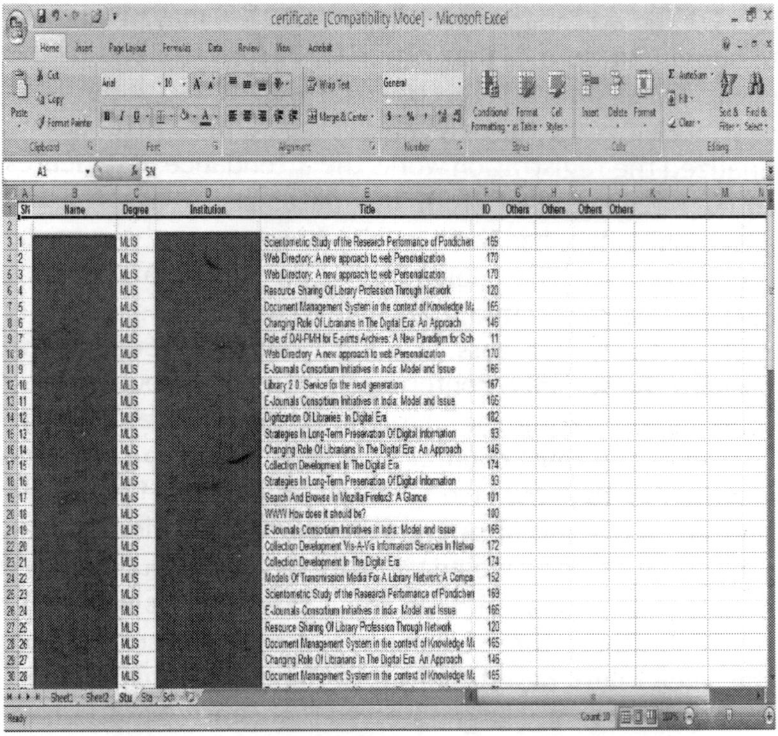

SN	Name	Degree	Institution	Title	ID	Others	Others	Others	Others
1		MLIS		Scientometric Study of the Research Performance of Pondicherr	169				
2		MLIS		Web Directory: A new approach to web Personalization	170				
3		MLIS		Web Directory: A new approach to web Personalization	170				
4		MLIS		Resource Sharing Of Library Profession Through Network	120				
5		MLIS		Document Management System in the context of Knowledge Ma	165				
6		MLIS		Changing Role Of Librarians In The Digital Era: An Approach	146				
7		MLIS		Role of OAI-PMH for E-prints Archives: A New Paradigm for Sch	11				
8		MLIS		Web Directory: A new approach to web Personalization	170				
9		MLIS		E-Journals Consortium Initiatives in India: Model and Issue	166				
10		MLIS		Library 2.0: Service for the next generation	167				
11		MLIS		E-Journals Consortium Initiatives in India: Model and Issue	106				
12		MLIS		Digitization Of Libraries: In Digital Era	182				
13		MLIS		Strategies In Long-Term Preservation Of Digital Information	93				
14		MLIS		Changing Role Of Librarians In The Digital Era: An Approach	146				
15		MLIS		Collection Development In The Digital Era	174				
16		MLIS		Strategies In Long-Term Preservation Of Digital Information	93				
17		MLIS		Search And Browse In Mozilla Firefox3: A Glance	101				
18		MLIS		WWW How does it should be?	100				
19		MLIS		E-Journals Consortium Initiatives in India: Model and Issue	166				
20		MLIS		Collection Development Vis-A-Vis Information Services In Netwo	172				
21		MLIS		Collection Development In The Digital Era	174				
22		MLIS		Models Of Transmission Media For A Library Network: A Compa	152				
23		MLIS		Scientometric Study of the Research Performance of Pondicherr	169				
24		MLIS		E-Journals Consortium Initiatives in India: Model and Issue	166				
25		MLIS		Resource Sharing Of Library Profession Through Network	120				
26		MLIS		Document Management System in the context of Knowledge Ma	165				
27		MLIS		Changing Role Of Librarians In The Digital Era: An Approach	146				
28		MLIS		Document Management System in the context of Knowledge Ma	165				

Screen Shot 3.21.4.5 Certificates-List of authors (Students)

Sometimes an author may have more than more than one paper. In such a case the decision would be taken by the authorities of the event as to whether to issue a single certificate or multiple. However we need not worry about the number of certificates as our job is limited to generate the titles list for preparing the certificates only. Let the authorities to take the decision regarding the said things.

3.21.5. Routine Issue of the Attendance Certificates

Issuing the attendance certificates to the authors is an important task in any seminar/conference. The attendance certificates may be requested by the authors for their official purpose. Hence, preparing the said certificates for the authors, who have turned for the event are eligible to receive the attendance certificates, as they may need them to submit to their higher officials. Before the end of the event, the said certificates could be prepared so that we can distribute them to the delegates at the earliest. After having finalized the registration works the attendance certificates could be generated from the database. I opt for the provision, which has the capacity to generate the reports, requested by the delegates. Once the attendance certificates are printed, they may be kept on the authority desk for further process. The files which are generated to prepare the seminar/conference certificates could also be used for preparing the attendance certificates. The in-charge of the third counter may be deputed to verify the certificates to avoid errors. People at Counter 1 and 2 are limited to the job of preparation of the certificates. The other related works would be taken up by the counter three people. For a clear picture about the routines which are related to these three counters, it could be observed from the given table. Based on my experience with the seminar/ conference event, I have observed that nearly 17 tasks have been faced by the registration section people that could be clearly explored in the given table. Hope that the given table could help the readers of this book to gather a idea about the routines of the registration section and make them take up their works in the right track without feeling the burdens.

Table 3.21.4.6 Routine of the Registration Section

Sl. No.	Tasks	1st Counter		2nd Counter		3rd Counter	
		Yes	No	Yes	No	Yes	No
1.	System	✓		✓		✓	
2.	Manpower	✓		✓		✓	
3.	Number of Persons required	2		2		2	
4.	ID Verification	✓		✓		✓	

5. Authors without ID	✓			✓	✓	
6. Already Registered		✓	✓		✓	
7. Authors with ID		✓	✓		✓	
8. IT Skilled staff	✓		✓		✓	
9. Additional staff with/without IT Skills	✓		✓		✓	
10. Enquiries	✓		✓		✓	
11. Registration form	✓			✓		✓
12. Printed Receipt	✓		✓			✓
13. Seminar/ Conference kit		✓		✓	✓	
14. Presentation Certificate		✓		✓	✓	
15. Participant Certificate		✓		✓	✓	
16. Attendance Certificate		✓		✓	✓	
17. Getting signature from the Authors (*for sl.no. 14-16*)					✓	

3.22. STRUCTURING THE SEMINAR/CONFERENCE VOLUME

There is no need to handover the papers to the printing press people for bringing the seminar/conference volume. The works which are related to compiling the volume also could be done by our desk as we have enough data to process it. For printing and binding purpose only, we could approach the press people.

3.22.1. Size of the Volume

First we have to collect the details about the volume size which was preferred by the authorities. Usually A4 size format is adopted for designing the seminar/conference volume; hence the same size is adopted by me to compile the volume with the adequate data.

3.22.2. Items to be included into the Volume

The following things may be included in the seminar/ conference volume.

1. Editorial Board details
2. Preface
3. Contents
4. List of contributors
5. List of Themes
6. Abstract
7. Full Text
8. Author Index
9. Title Index
10. Subject Index
11. Authors' Address which includes phone and E-mail Ids.

3.22.2.1. Details of the Editorial Board

This section deals with the details of the editorial board members that include editors and associate editors, who are behind the compilation of the volume. Adequate details about the editorial board could be given here.

3.22.2.2. Preface

Preface always gives the outline of the document in which the coverage of the volume would be explored briefly.

3.22.2.3. Contents

The contents are a must in any document that gives

enough details on the papers which are included in the volume. It is a must to prepare the contents on the basis of the theme structure and that should be matched with the titles of the papers also. I have generated the report of contents in which the themes are indexed in ascending format and under the themes; all the titles are sequenced according to the author index. The classified indexing system is adopted here to group the titles which are related to the themes (7 themes) and the related authors also sequenced in alphabetical order. The given sketch and the screen shot enable you to capture the classification system which is incorporated to generate the required output in the contents section.

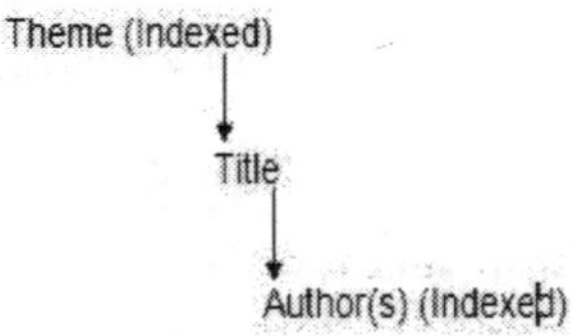

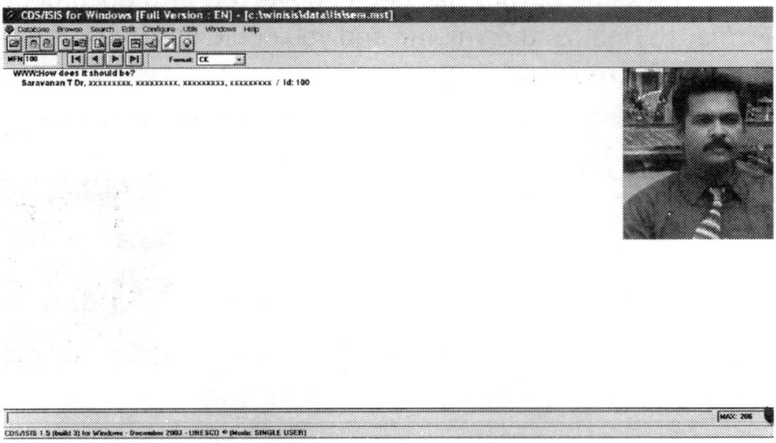

Screen Shot 3.22.2.3.1 Content List

Observe that the theme has not been shown in the above screen shot for ID:100. The title and the related authors have been displayed here. I have applied the sorting concept which is one of the features of the WinISIS® that make our jobs easier to take the output as given below which you are looking for here. The generated given output shows the theme details.

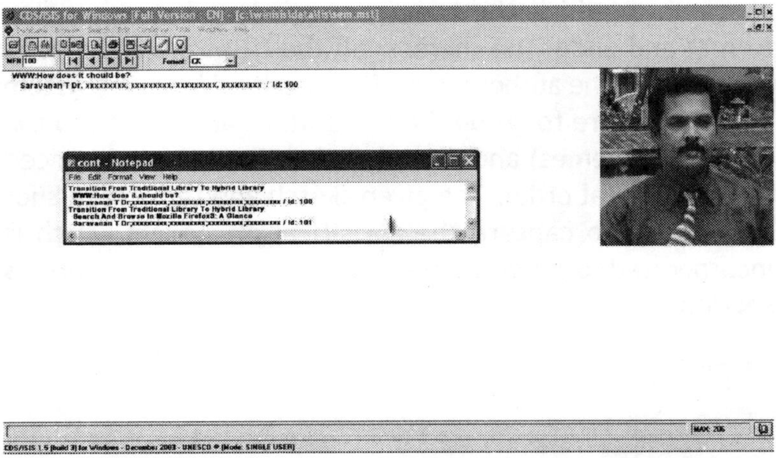

Screen Shot 3.22.2.3.2 Content List in Text format

The same output has been converted into document format to finalize the volume and you could observe it from the given screen shot.

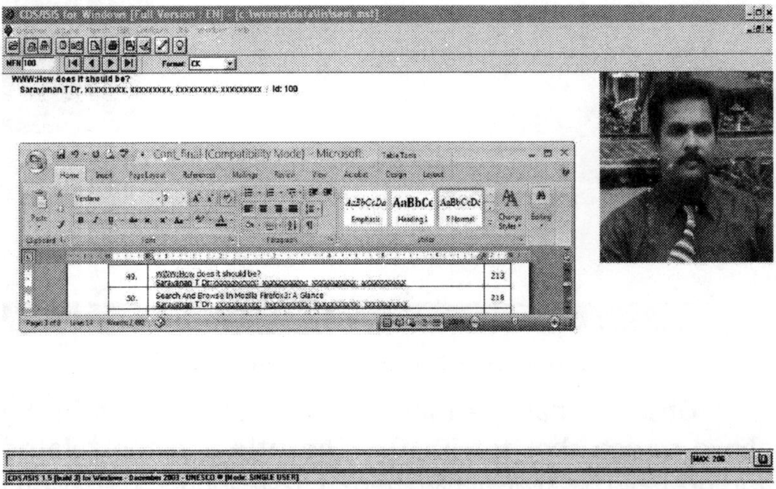

Screen Shot 3.22.2.3.3 Content List in Document format

The exported data has been structured with the help of grid format that could be observed from the above screen shot. There are exactly 3 columns as it would have been structured for the content of the volume. First column denotes the serial number of the papers; second column includes the details on Titles, Author(s). Look at the given screen shot where the third column contains the page number. The data have been arranged in a grid format that gives an attractive look of the output. However, these settings are our optional and the grid settings may or may not be adopted depending on your local choices. The data which you are looking for on the text/document format as above could also be structured using the spread sheet format where you have the grid and column format that make our works easier. The spread sheet based output could be transferred into the document where you are structuring your seminar/ conference volume.

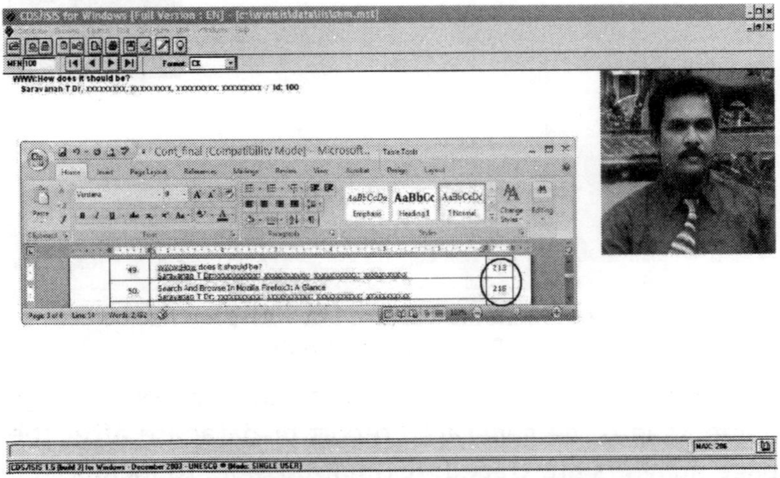

Screen Shot 3.22.2.3.4 Content List with page numbers

There are two ways to fix the page numbers in the content area. They are

1. After having finalized the contents and paper

arrangements, the textual page numbers would be identified manually that could be done by a team of faculty members after having a cross check with the pages where the related titles exist. Once the verifications are finalised the page numbers could be entered directly into the generated output not into the database.

2. Another option is after tracing the page numbers of titles the numbers could be fed into the database by editing the concerned record using author Id. You can generate the report along with the page numbers when you have the data in the authors' record.

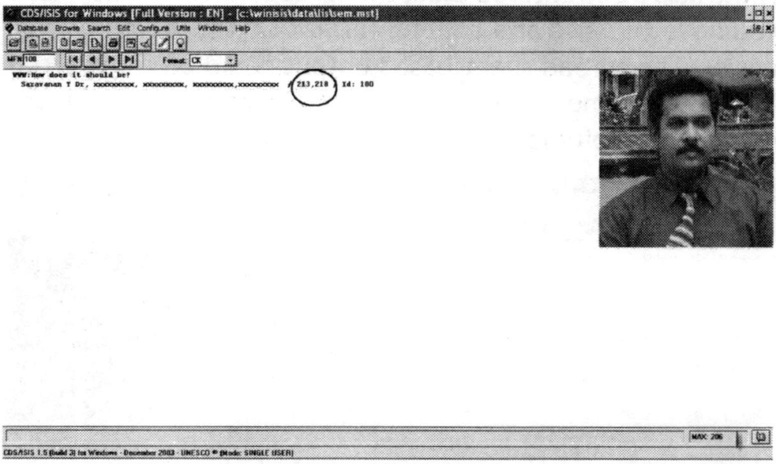

Screen Shot 3.22.2.3.5 Content List with page numbers (Database generated)

However, in both the cases you could enter the page numbers into the generated report or database after the page numbers are traced. It is not possible to include the page number details also when entering the bibliographic details of the papers into the database at the beginning.

Let us observe the given screen shot which explores the content details along with the page numbers as the database has the page numbers in the concerned author ID:100, and in other Ids, if any. Now we could take the report along with page numbers as observed from the screen shot.

3.22.2.4. List of Contributors

The list of contributors could be generated in an ascending format that enables the readers to locate the authors and the related papers. Here the list of contributors includes all the authors even if they are co-authors. Index plays major role in any kind of data organization. Hence, I adopt three indexing systems that could be usually identified as Title index, Author index and Subject index so that volume would get more strength when it comes to the final structure.

The contributors' details which have been indexed could be viewed from the following report.

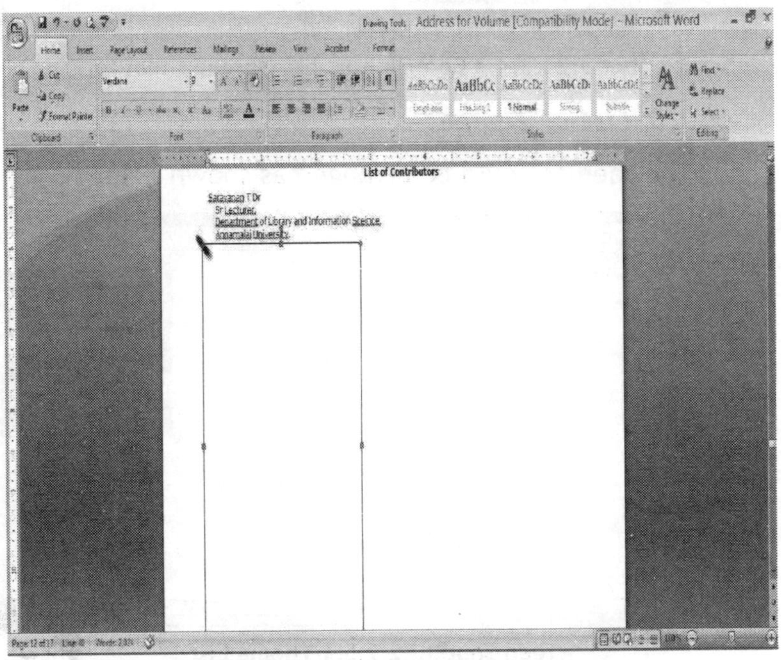

Screen Shot 3.22.2.4.1 Contributors list (document format)

The contributors' details could be generated towards the spread sheet format makes our works easy and compact. The given screen shot explores the same above from a different angle.

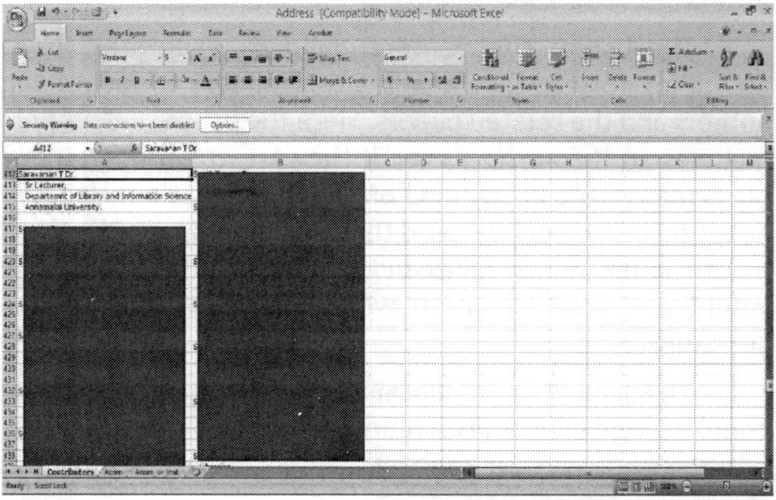

Screen Shot 3.22.2.4.2 Contributors list (spread sheet format)

3.22.2.5. List of Themes

The themes could be arranged as shown below.

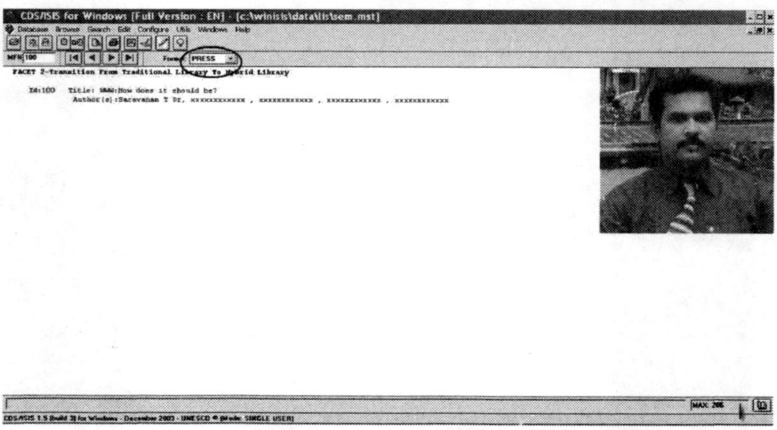

Screen Shot 3.22.2.5.1 Theme List

Let us observe the given screen shot which explores the exported data output towards text mode in which the data shown in the database output could be generated as it is.

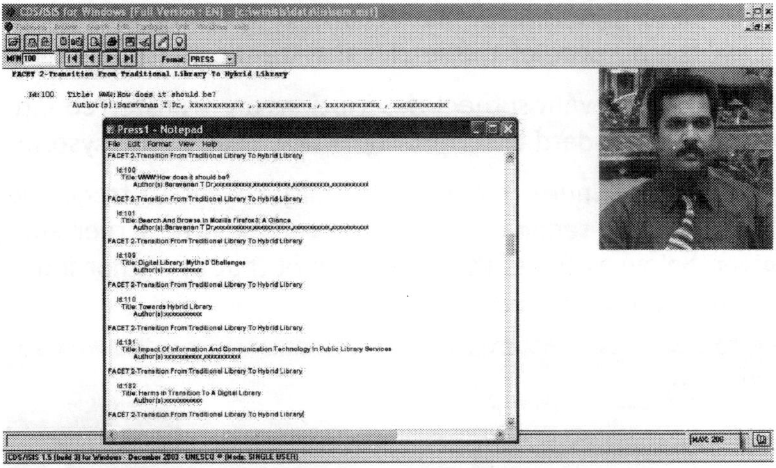

Screen Shot 3.22.2.5.2 Theme List in Text format

Compiling press format has been discussed in the previous sections with required details.

3.22.2.6. Abstract

Abstract could be collected from the electronic copy which have been sent by the authors to our desk. Change the format of the abstract as per our requirements and keep them in sequence.

3.22.2.7. Full Text

Full text of the document also could be collected from the electronic copy in the same way as discussed in the Abstract. Change the format of the Full Text as per our requirements and keep them in sequence.

3.22.2.8. Author Index

Vickery has pointed out that there are three stages in indexing system. They are

a. The text is scanned to select a set of words, phrases or sentences which collectively represent its subject.

b. A decision is taken as to which of these subject descriptions are worth recording as being relevant to the purpose of the retrieval system.

c. The relevant subject descriptions are transferred into the standard descriptor language used in the system.

Author index is one of the major ways to trace the authors in the seminar/conference volume. The screen shot given below explores the generated output of author index towards the text mode.

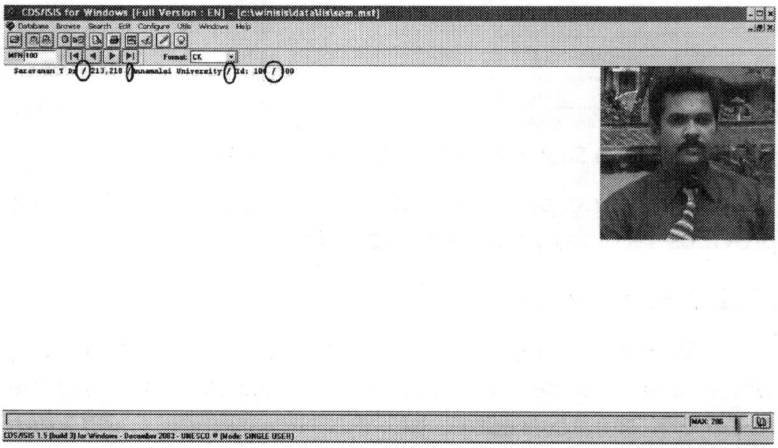

Screen Shot 3.22.2.8.1 Author Index with separator

The separator '/' has been used to split the data which could be observed from the above screen shot. When there is a need to export the data into another format, these kinds of separators are essential ones. Symbol preference is our choice as we are the designers of the database. I have used the said symbol in the database to extract the required data. From the above output you could capture that along with the author name, pages and Institution, the authors' ID and the fee details are also explored that could be removed after the conversion and verification of the data. The converted format of the author index would be viewed with reference to the given screen shot.

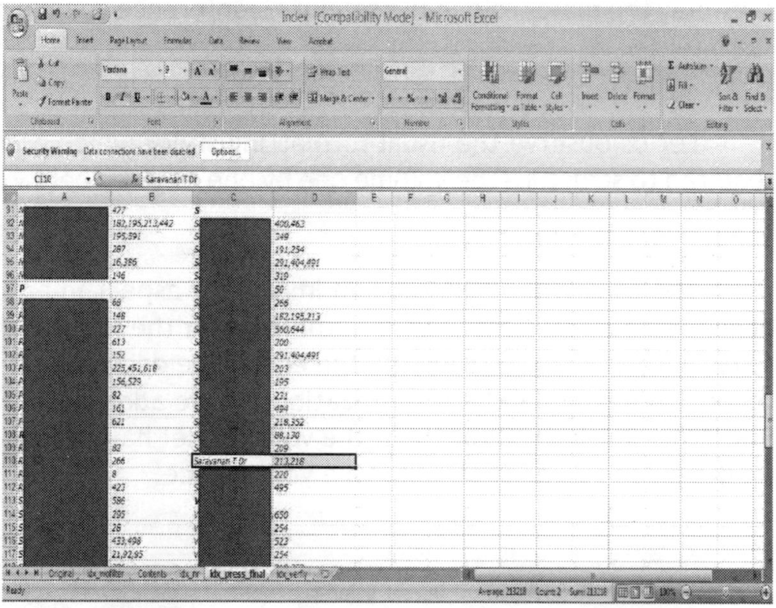

Screen Shot 3.22.2.8.2 Author Index with page numbers

All the authors that include the co-authors also have been arranged in an ascending order under the alphabets shown above. Here the separator '/' I have used to extract the author name (Saravanan T Dr) along with the page numbers (213,218). The author ID and the Fee 500/- are removed from the output which are explored in the *Screen Shot 3.22.2.8.1.*

3.22.2.9. Title Index

Apart from the author index one more indexing system known as Title index has been structured to access the required data in the volume. This index also offers the feature to locate the required data in the volume. Hence both types of indexing system could be adopted for better performance of the volume. Remember that nothing should be ignored while structuring the index for the volume. Standardization must be adopted to design the indexes, as they play the major role in the seminar/conference volume.

3.23. FONTS

Let us observe the usual formatting styles which are required to structure the volume one by one as given below.

3.23.1. Set the Font Type

The font type is perhaps an important aspect in any document output. Consult your authorities for the font type selection and keep the same till the end of the document to secure uniformity and standardization. I have adopted the font type 'Vardana' throughout the volume. Let have a look on the given screen shot and make your choice.

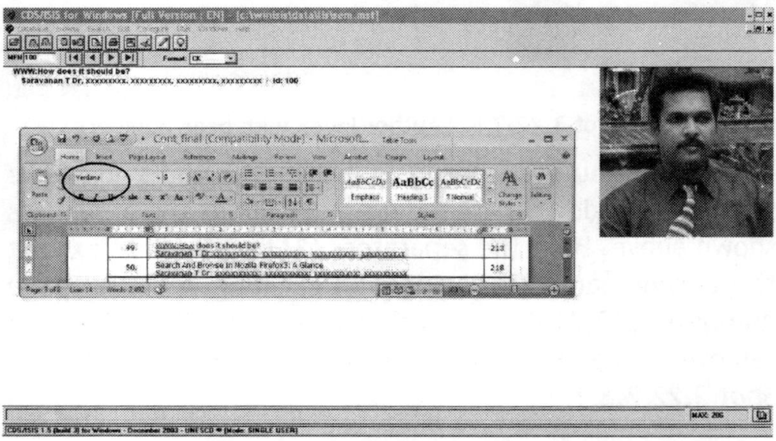

Screen Shot 3.23.1 Font Type

3.23.2. Set the Font Size

Like the font type the size also is a major thing that helps to fix the number of pages of the document output. When the font size increases the length of the page also would be increased as it occupies more spaces in the line set. Hence, take the sample output for a page with different font size and get the approval from your authorities. However the Headings and the Sub headings should have a greater size than the full text. Setting the colour options for various headings and important areas are purely optional that may be decided by your authorities. I have adopted the font size 11 for Headings, subheadings and 9 for the full text throughout the volume. Observe the given screen shot and make your own choice.

Attention: *Remember that the formats which have been structured by you in the seminar/conference volume must be accepted by the editorial desk as they have the complete rights to make/cancel any decisions. Hence, finalize your work after getting the approval from their desk.*

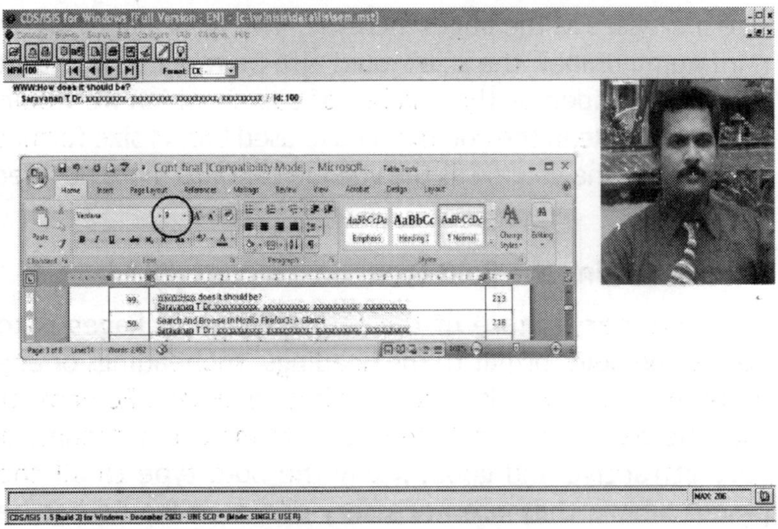

Screen Shot 3.23.2 Font Size

3.23.3. Set the Line Space

Line space between the lines gives neatness to the document and it should not have more space lines. Many of the volumes I found that they have used single line space between the lines and it may cause some inconvenience to the readers of those documents to capture and follow up the lines. Readers' eyes should not be put to severe task. Better to give single lines for the abstract part only. I have adopted line space 1 for the abstract part and 1.5 line space throughout the volume. Make your own choice.

3.23.4. Setting the Margins

The standard left, right, top and bottom margins could be adopted to structure the volume.

3.23.5. Setting the Page Size

The page size of the volume would differ from event to event. I have never seen any standardization among the size of the page in many events. The size of the pages may or may not be decided based on the number of pages. The size increases as the pages increase. When the pages are in minimum number, the size would also be reduced and that could be decided by the number of papers which we would like to compile in the volume. I have used the A4 size format to bring out the volume as the volume contains more number of pages.

3.23.6. Setting the Bold Type

Another feature of the text editing packages is to define the Bold format to the headings, subheadings or any other important words, wherever it is necessary. Remember that these settings would help us all to make our document very attractive and good. Apply the Bold type to all the places where they are necessary one as it would not be decent if applied throughout the volume. Simple but neat arrangements with the required settings would always take the document to a high level slot and attract others. I have applied the 'Bold' to all headings and sub headings only. Make your own suitable choice.

3.23.7. Setting the Italics Style

Italics style could be usually applied in the Bibliography/Reference areas to follow up the cataloguing rules which exist at international standard. Hence, the said style may be applied, wherever it is applicable and that could be decided by you. Though there are many works related to the seminar/conference volumes, some of the major settings which are concerned with the documents have been discussed earlier. There may or may not be choices to face the local variations and based on that make your own choice.

3.24. VALIDATIONS REQUIRED BEFORE FINALISING THE SEMINAR/CONFERENCE VOLUME

Be sure about the structure of the document. Otherwise allow the whole compilation jobs related to the volume to the press professionals as more care is needed to structure the volume. The volume compilation in our desk may help the organizers to reduce the expense which is actually required for the press works. In many of the seminar/conference events, the volume compilation jobs are handed over to the press professionals as they do not prefer to take the responsibility for compiling the volume. However, in the indexing part press professionals alone never finalize it without having consultations with us. We do not expect more outputs from the press professionals beyond the limits. If you are sure to carry out the task, go through the given validation process before finalising the compilation.

3.24.1. Cross Check I

Once the compilations are finalised in our desk, the volume may be handed over to the press professionals towards the electronic format for taking the final copy. Any works which are related with the volume required the proof mode so as errors could be avoided and without which further process is not possible as it requires more attention and verifications. Ask the press people to give the proof of the volume which is structured by us. Verify the sections such as editorial area, preface, contents and contributors, etc, inside the volume.

3.24.2. Cross Check II

After the section verifications, the page numbers which are existing in the pages should be entered in the content page and in the index part. Remember that the page numbers which exist in each page could be allotted by the press people and not by us as the press format sometimes varies from our desktop settings. Hence, better not allot the page number in our desk while compiling the volume and let the press people to carry out the task. Now, it is our responsibility to trace the page numbers and prepare the indexing parts for the final version of the volume.

Attention: *Remember that the page number systems which have been discussed in the earlier sections could have been done over and above the said press process. Whether entering the page numbers into the database or directly into the volume contents/indexes could be possible after getting the proof format from the press.*

3.24.3. Cross Check III

Handover the contents and all the printed pages, which have passed the second cross check to a team consisting of two members who are working for the seminar/conference, and request them to cross check with the contents and the papers. One person may have the content list on his desk and the other one would be responsible for the papers.

Attention: *In our event, the number of pages in the proof has gone beyond 1000 pages. The first person who has the content list could read the first title followed by the first author, second author, if any, and so on. Moreover the first* *person may use any of the identification marks once the title is read out. The second person who is responsible for the full texts could verify the details which have been read out by the first person and make the corrections if anything exists. Completed pages could be marked by the second person also. The said process could be taken till the end of the pages of the proof mode. It is the duty of the said team to verify the page numbers also which are found in the content area.*

3.24.4. Cross Check IV

After having successfully finalized the verification concerning with the contents, page numbers, title of the papers, authors names the whole content part may be handed over to some other persons for further verification. The team who are involved previously for the verification purpose should be called again for this process. A new team consisting of two people must carry out the same works which have been taken in the Third cross check to ensure accuracy of the data. A clear instruction is a must to the team who have been involved in these sections as it is the major task which should not receive any undesirable errors. Let us observe the given screen shot which enables you to carry out the way of cross checking in the proof copy.

We are all familiar that any kind of data could be accessed by using the indexing systems. But here in contrary the index part could be fixed towards the pages as the exact page numbers would be located on the pages only and from there we may move to an index part to fix the page numbers. Remember that here the indexing works could not be finalized and are only under process. Tracing the data towards the index is not possible at that time. So any indexing part could not be properly utilized to trace the required data without finalizing it. Now ask the first person from a team to take the first page of the paper and read the first author name. It is the duty of the other person from the same team to locate the exact name in the Indexing part that could be done easily as it has been already indexed. Instruct to the second person to write the page number against the author name to find whether it would be matched. Ask them to continue the same process till all the papers are exhausted. If any doubts are raised or errors committed, check them again immediately and clear them. Remember that works should not be interrupted or postponed under any circumstances. After having fed the page numbers into the content, the Index part which would be handed over to the press people in the form of word/pdf to carry out the final job.

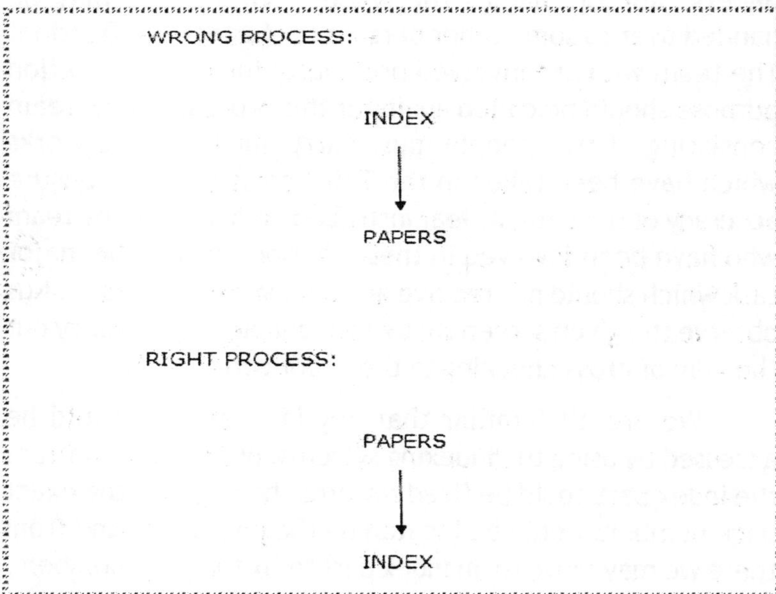

Screen Shot 3.24.1 Validation method

Attention: *While doing this process or after the process don't try to add or remove any thing from the corrected volume as any new additions/deletions would collapse the entire process. Further, we don't have more time to carry out the cross check again to ensure accuracy* *as we have to deal with more number of pages that would definitely cause problems to ensure data accuracy.*

3.25. OTHER DATABASES

Apart from the 'Sem.Mst' database some more databases have been structured and utilized by the way of RDBMS concept and also it is one of the features of WinISIS® that made me to complete the task easily without much burden. The relational concept has enabled me to organized the data in a nice way so as I could fulfil the requirements of the authority of the event. When organizing the data which exist in more numbers, this kind of architecture is an essential one that could be possible with any of the advanced data mining packages that exist in the IT field. Here, I have explored some of the other databases (*not all the sets*) which are interacted from the master database 'Sem.Mst' and other related sets (*These sets have not been discussed here briefly as the E-R concepts require advanced level of database knowledge, which may confuse the general readers of this book*). A few samples are;

3.25.1 Database for the Transport section *(Tnprt.mst)*

3.25.2 Database for the Accommodation section *(Acm.mst)*

3.25.3 Database for the Food section *(Food.mst)*

3.25.4 Database for the Decorations section *(Decn.mst)*

3.25.5 Database for the Gift section *(Gift.mst)*

3.25.1 Database for the Transport section *(Tnprt.mst)*:

This database has been formulated to maintain the details about the transport committee that includes the following fields. It is a must to formulate a committee like this to assist the delegates during the event. Depending, on the requirement, the manpower could be allotted for the transport jobs, which is an unavoidable routine. Under this concern, the details of the committee members could be maintained with the help of this database so that we could generate any kind of report as and when required.

Id

Name

Designation

Address

Phone

E-mail

Visual

3.25.2. Database for the Accommodation Section *(Acm.mst)*

This database has been formulated to maintain the details about the Accommodation committee that includes the following fields. When the delegates prefer the accommodation, it is our responsibility to give enough details about their location on our premises along with accommodation in charge details and that could be generated from the following database.

Id

Name

Designation

Address

Phone

E-mail

Visual

3.25.3. Database for the Database for the Food Section *(Food.mst):*

A database has been formulated to maintain the details about the Food committee that includes the following fields. This kind of committee is also an important one to carry out the food related arrangements. The duties which are related with the food arrangement could be informed to the concerned members by letter/E-mail which might be generated from our database.

Id

Name

Designation

Address

Phone

E-mail

Visual

3.25.4. Database for the Decorations Section *(Decn.mst)*

This database has been formulated to maintain the details about the Decoration committee with following fields. The said committee would take the responsibilities to decorate the places where the events have been scheduled. Many of the duties concerned with this section could be informed properly to the members via our database generated reports so that they could know their routines in the event.

Id

Name

Designation

Address

Phone

E-mail

Visual

3.25.5. Database for the Gift section *(Gift.mst)*

This database has been formulated to maintain the details about the Gift committee that includes the following fields. These are some of the routines in any event; hence much importance is given to this section. Required gift items should be carefully finalized, then informed to the members of the committee for further action as their role would go on till the end of the event.

Id

Name

Designation

Address

Phone

E-mail

Visual

Attention: *Remember that the structured committee people should not be interchanged as per our requirement that would violate the data organization and also against the principles of management. The person should carry out the works which have been allotted by the committee in which he/she is working. Other committee related works should not be exchanged on any other committee under any circumstances. Let them carry out their committee related jobs only so that we could bring out good performance of the event. However, the works which are related with the other sections are beyond the limits of this book.*

3.26. DATABASE SECURITY

3.26.1. Backup

Abraham Silberschatz (et al) has brought out some of the global routine maintenance activities for the Database Administrators and they could be observed under the sub heading '*for database designers*' from the chapter 6.

The duties of any database designer is not only limited to the design and organization of the database. Designer has to take care about the security of the data which exists in the database as the works have consumed more time and energy of the database designer. The time taken was by me to organize the data for the seminar is more than three months. Imagine that if anything would happen to the database, who will take care of it? The data security may result in any of the following items;

a. Data Loss

b. Database Loss

When the data is organized with modern technology in electronic format, there may or may not be a chance to face the said two incidents which could occur at any time whatever the infrastructure we have on our desk. As everyone is familiar about the data backup system, which may be one of the methods to secure them. I followed the same backup method and the data backup was taken by me every day after the works have been finished. The import and export options which are available in the database may enable us to carry out the said process. In any available database system you may see the same feature as they are essential for any database organization.

3.26.2. Access Code to Open the Database

The data error and the database security problem may happen when the database would be accessed by unauthorized persons. Remember that the person who is not related with the database job should not be allowed to enter your circle to operate the database. Otherwise any wrong operation and access would always cause unnecessary problems to your desk and this kind of environment also should be avoided. Hence it is better you use the password option to access the database. Password system is the most popular in any kind of electronic data organization. Hence, I have adopted the same process to access the 'Sem' database which was structured by me for the seminar and without my knowledge no one could access the database.

Attention: *Remember that though you have used the password system to access the database which has been created using WinISIS® application, it could also be accessed by someone who is an expert in the same application. But, it is tough for others, who are not experts in WinISIS® application. If you need full security for your database, you have to write an additional program by using the ISIS Pascal programming option or an external programming library, the ISIS_DLL* for the higher version of WinISIS® that requires high level programming knowledge.*

*ISIS_DLL is an External Programming Library which is developed by BIREME/PAHO and UNESCO. The sources can be downloaded from the UNESCO's website www.unesco.org/isis and BIREME's website named as www.bireme.br.

You can get more information from the given screen shot which has been structured by me to access the database.

Screen Shot 3.26.2 Access the database

The above option lets you to open the database when it matches the access code which is entered by you or else you have to quit from it in case if the access code is not matched which is the common routine expected at the gate of any database system. Defining the password option usually differs from database to database that could be learned by having continuous interaction with the tool in which you would like to structure your data.

3.26.3. Pascal Program

However, as I have already discussed above, the password option will be broken, if someone is an expert in WinISIS® package. To avoid this kind of insecurity, I have used the Pascal external programs which can be incorporated into our database so as the restrictions are possible for any of the unauthorized access and keep others away from our circle. Remember that writing the Pascal programs require a high level programming knowledge. If you are an advanced user of the ISIS package and having programming skills in Pascal, then go ahead or else seek someone who is close to you for writing the programs as per your requirements.

From the screen shot 3.26.2, which lets us enter the access code to open WinISIS® database will verify the password which has been entered by us. If the code is accepted we will be directed to the given screen shot which is created using the Pascal program where you have to enter another access code for further action. Let us observe the given screen shot which has been structured by using the Pascal program which secures the database from unauthorized access.

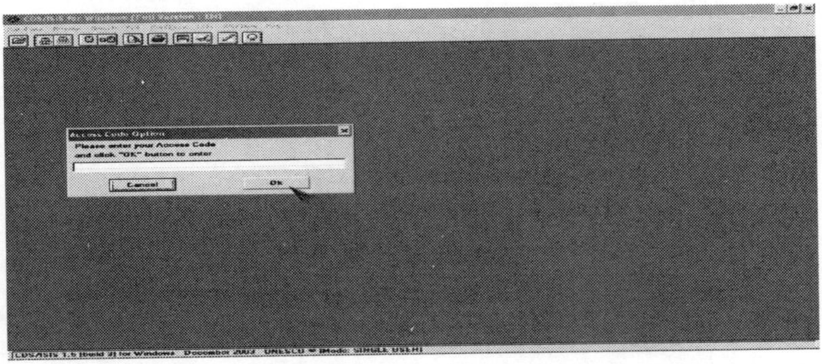

Screen Shot 3.26.3.1 Password Dialog

The above option requires the access code to enter into the database. If you enter any wrong access code, you will be directed to the screen shot which is given below.

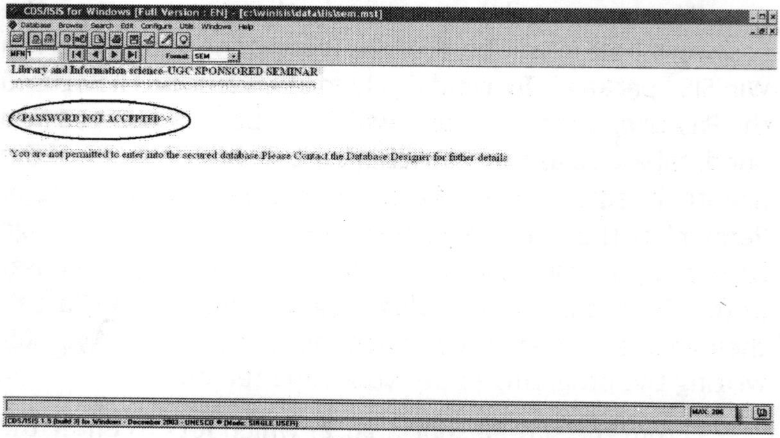

Screen Shot 3.26.3.2 Wrong Password

So you will not be permitted to view the data without entering the right password at the entry gate. Once the password is matched you will be taken to the screen shot which is given below where you can see the message 'PASSWORD ACCEPTED' which has been clearly displayed inside the oval shape.

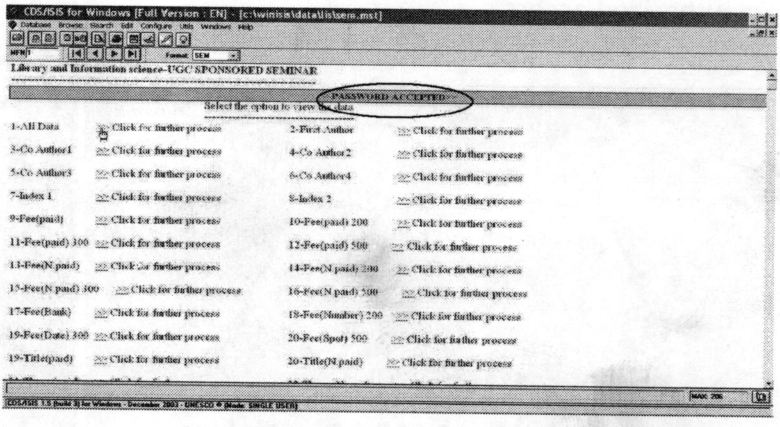

Screen Shot 3.26.3.3 Right Password

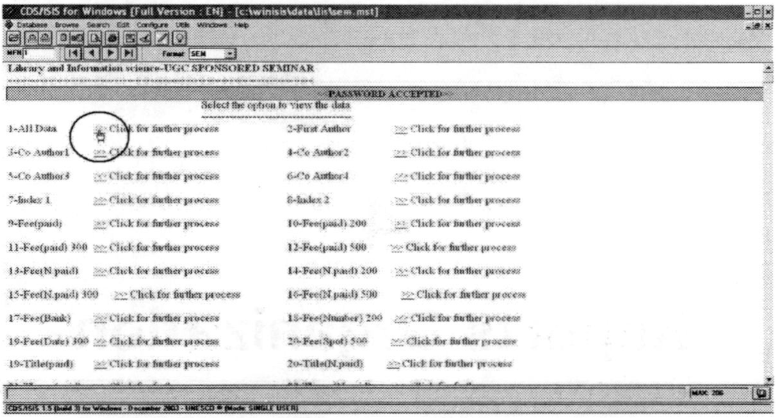

Screen Shot 3.26.3.4 Accessing Print formats i

The above screen contains all the print formats which have helped me to access the data in various structures by way of clicking the required option which has been shown within the circle which is also displayed on the above screen shot for better capture. When we move the cursor of the mouse on the symbol '>>', the icon will be changed as given in the above screen shot. Let us observe the following screen shot where the clicking options have been highlighted. When we click these options we will be directed to the required outputs.

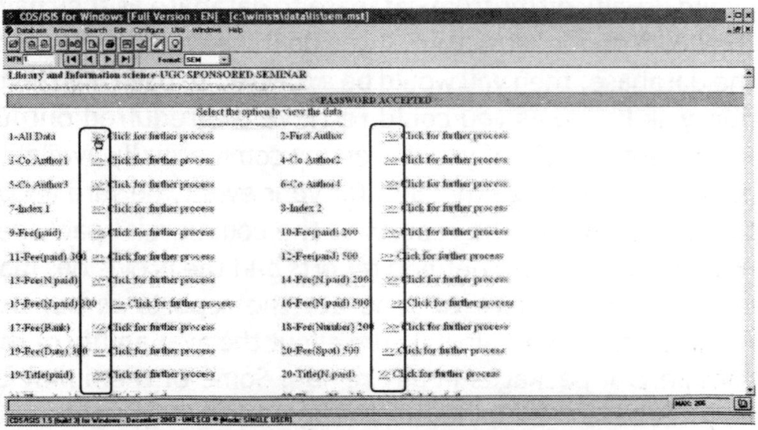

Screen Shot 3.26.3.5 Accessing Print formats ii

4

Reports Organization

Reports are the essential things, which are playing the important role in any kind of information architecture. Without reports the purpose of using the modern tools are meaningless. The structured data could be viewed towards the report, as it offers multiple features to the designers as well as others. For any kind of database related tasks, the reports are unavoidable things, which could be one of the best ways to realize our works which have been carried out by us with the structured database. The report generation would usually differ from database to database as they have their own queries structure. If you deal the data directly with the database, then you would be expected to have high level query skills, so as you could retrieve the required output from the database. If you prefer any commercially available package to organize the data for your event, be sure about the availability of the reports as the commercial packages usually have the pre defined reports and the provisions may or may not be there to generate the reports as per our requirements. But I am not sure about the availability of the commercial packages in any region. Some of them may or may not have their in house packages for their purpose only and they may or may not come for commercial purpose. If you are an experienced person in the database sectors, you need not depend on any one or commercial packages for the data organization as you may develop your own database by using any of the available database tools in which you are experienced.

In this book, I have generated the reports towards the package WinISIS® as I have discussed in the previous chapters that the package has the feature to structure any kind of output by defining the simple programs (in WinISIS®, these are referred to as print formats) and also the package offers the sub fields and repeatable fields features which are such wonderful things to manipulate any kind of data. When we use the commercial packages to access the data towards its front end, some restrictions are there to generate the report. But if you deal the data directly with the database without the front end any kind of report generation would be possible but it requires the skills to define the queries. Let us observe the given examples which may help you to understand the difference among the queries when we adopt various databases.

4.1. ADDRESS (FIRST AUTHOR ONLY)

The first author address has been generated here from the database..

Id - 100 Saravanan T Dr,
Sr.Lecturer,
Department of Library and Information Science,
Annamalai University,Annamalainagar,
Chidambaram-Cuddalore Dt,
Tamilnadu-608 002-INDIA.

The above report has been done by using the simple print format commands which have been written by me in

WinISIS® package so as that could be made possible. The ID:100 includes one main author and four co-authors. As the feature of sub field option which is available in WinISIS® package enabled me to extract the data by using the given print format. Look at the given sample format which is used to generate the above output.

4.1.1. Print format of WinISIS®

```
If p(v1) then {fs20,'Id -'}, v1,fi,if p(v2) then
c8,v2,',',fi,/c8,if p(v3^a) then v3^a,',' else if p(v3^b) then
c8,v3^b',' else if p(v3^c) then c8,v3^c,',',fi,fi,fi/ c8,v4,','/
c8,if p(v8^c) then v8^c,',',fi/c8,if p(v8^d) then v8^d,',',fi/
c8,if p(v8^e) then v8^e,',',fi /c8,if p(v8^f) then v8^f,',',fi/
c8,if p(v8^g) then v8^g,',' fi/c8,if p(v8^h) then v8^h, ',',fi/
##
```

The same output could be generated using MsAccess® database but, defining the query would be differed.

4.1.2. Query in MsAccess®

A select query is a type of database object that shows information in Datasheet view. A query can get its data from one or more tables, from existing queries, or from a combination of the two. Defining query in SQL® or ORACLE® or MsAccess® requires advanced level of experience for preparing good reports as well as to avoid errors.

```
Select id, autname1, design, dept, ins, dno, st, place,
city, dt, state, country, pin from Table_name1 ,
Table_name2, Table_name3,Table_name4 where
Table_name1.id=100 and Table_ name 1 .id=Table_name2.id
and Table_name1.id=Table_name3.id and Table_name1.id =
Table_ name4.id order by Table_name1.id;
```

See *Annexure-iv,* which contains an advanced level of a sample query that would generate the report for all the authors. The said sample query has been used in an application named as '**CSbyTS**' *(Annexure-iii)*, which is developed by me and a total solution for the seminars and conference events. However, the features of this application are not discussed here as they are beyond the limitations of this book.

Observe the above query which has been structured as sample for the generation of address report for the first author who is in the ID:100. The query has included four tables as they have adopted the relational concept. The primary key and foreign key concepts are required here to generate the report as above. For an instance, I have written the above query by which you could realize the difference of various queries which exist in every package. The relational concepts are perhaps the same in all the packages. But defining the fields may differ which depends on the package rules and regulations.

Like that, you could use Oracle® database also to organize the data and it is possible to generate the report as said above. Remember that when you prefer the Ms Access® or Oracle®, advanced skill in the database sector is a must and also these databases are all case sensitive tools as you should take care while extracting the data from the database. When you prefer the Ms Access® or Oracle®, the reports could be taken towards the Crystal Report® designer which offers wonderful solution that could be possible when you have expertise in it. Here I don't have any discussion about the Oracle® output or Crystal Report® designer as my choice has differed. There are many reference sources that exist in the market to get the familiarity in the database. Make your choice.

Let me explore the various forms of reports, which are generated from the database which has been created to organize the data. Nearly 42 print formats have been created by me to generate the required report. The table which is displayed here would enable you to capture necessary information about the reports and also realize the necessity of the reports.

4.2. PRINT FORMATS STRUCTURED IN THE DATABASE

Sl.No.	Reports	Description	Index
1.	Full Format	All data display	Yes
2.	Author 1	First author details	Yes
3.	Author 2	First Co-Author details	Yes
4.	Author 3	Second Co-Author details	Yes
5.	Author 4	Third Co-Author details	Yes
6.	Author 5	Fourth Co-Author details	Yes
7.	Author Index 1	Ascending pattern	Yes
8.	Author Index 2	Ascending pattern	Relative Index
9.	Fee 200	Fee for Students (Paid)	Yes
10.	Fee 300	Fee for Scholars (Paid)	Yes
11.	Fee 500	Fee for Staff (Paid)	Yes
12.	Fee	Fee for all categories (Paid)	Yes
13.	Fee 200	Fee for Students (Not Paid)	Yes
14.	Fee 300	Fee for Scholars (Not Paid)	Yes
15.	Fee 500	Fee for Staff (Not Paid)	Yes
16.	Fee	Fee for all categories (Not Paid)	Yes
17.	Fee	Bank wise	Yes
18.	Fee	Number wise	Yes
19.	Fee	Date wise	Yes
20.	Fee	Spot Registration	Yes
21.	Titles	For Registered authors	Yes
22.	Titles	For Not Registered authors	Yes
23.	Themes	For Registered authors	Classified System

24.	Themes	For Not Registered authors	Classified System
25.	Contents	For Registered authors	Classified System
26.	Index	For Registered authors	Classified System
27.	Address	For Registered authors	Yes
28.	Accommodation	First Location	Yes
29.	Accommodation	Second Location	Yes
30.	Accommodation	Third Location	Yes
31.	Gender	Male and Female	Yes
32.	Volume	Press format	Yes
33.	Letters	Reply to all authors	No
34.	Letters	For Transport Committee	No
35.	Letters	For Food Committee	No
36.	Letters	For Decoration Committee	No
37.	Letters	For Accommodation Committee	No
38.	Letters	For Gift/other works Committee	No
39.	Titles	For Certificates	Yes
40.	Contributors	List of authors with address for the volume	Yes
41.	Phone number	To maintain author cell/phone numbers	Yes
42.	E-mail Id	To maintain author e-mail details	Yes

The above listed print formats have been used to generate the various reports which are required to organize the seminar with full compact. Apart from the listed report possibilities, are there to make more outputs that depend on our requirements. The reports which I would have formulated to organize the seminar may or may not suit to your environment and make your choice to structure the outputs. There is no limit to generate the report as per our needs, as WinISIS® offers this feature that could be utilized properly so that the power of the package could be realized.

5

Problems Identified

Akotia established that ICT was considered an indispensable tool for enhancing productivity throughout any of the country. Further he noted that many organizations had lacked staff who understood the functional requirements for recordkeeping with the competencies and skills required to manage electronic information delivery systems. Stephen M. Mutula and Justus M. Wamukoya traced some other problems that were identified as impeding automation of archives and consequent management of electronic records were:

- Lack of prioritisation of automation functions and services;
- Lack of policies and guidelines;
- Lack of awareness among records personnel about e-records management;
- Lack of knowledge;
- Lack of competencies;
- Lack of skills;
- Lack of standards, practices and procedures for the management of e-records;

- Lack of long-term preservation;
- Inability to determine appropriate hardware and software.

Keakopa noted that in eastern and southern Africa, agencies with statutory responsibility for records were adopting new technologies without any clear strategy for managing the information created.

According to ICA, the speed at which information technologies and e-records have been adopted around the world and particularly in developing countries, has left little opportunity to develop and institute internationally or nationally accepted standards or practice. Standards in e-records management are important or selecting information technology infrastructure, ensuring security of records, and validating data and records.

Wamukoya and Mutula point out that in the eastern and southern Africa region, electronic records are being created in public institutions and some are being mismanaged and/ or lost.

I have experienced many problems while organising the data in various aspects for the seminar and they are explored here for your benefit so as these kinds of problems may be avoided in your boundaries.

5.1. PROBLEMS WITH AUTHORS ID

When the delegates send the full text via mail they may commit the mistakes in typing their ID which has been given from our desk. Hence, I was not able to receive their paper on time. They would not realize the necessity of the ID. With the help of other related bibliographic details, only these kinds of problems could be solved and the authors' exact ID is traced and the same might be informed to the authors immediately. Otherwise, during the time of the seminar/conference, the authors will come and stand in front of us for further enquiries with the wrong ID.

5.2. PROBLEMS WITH THE PAPERS

I received some mail which explores the details of the attached papers such as the title, author details, etc. But, when I downloaded the attached documents the details of the co-authors/institution/designation might not match with mail information which caused the confusion in the data process. The mismatch may be related to any of the following;

a. No uniformity in the titles
b. Misplacement of the co-authors
c. Contrary details of the designations
d. Misplacement of the first name and surname

5.3. PROBLEMS WITH THE DD

My desk received some DDs (Demand Draft) which were sent by the authors by post. The details such as DD number, Date, Bank's name might be informed by them to us via mail before the post arrived on our desk. But in some cases I received the mail about the details of the DD but did not receive the post within the scheduled time due to various reasons. These kinds of problems could be handled with care as it deals with finance.

5.4. PROBLEMS WITH THE ATTACHMENT

In some of the mails, I have not found the attachment of the full text paper but the mail states that the papers have been attached. What do we do? This problem might be caused while they attach the files to their mail. Unless the attachment job is finished the mail should not be communicated by the authors to our desk. Hence, it is our duty to inform the lack of attachment so that they could send another mail along with the required attached document to our desk. The dual process sometimes extends our work outside the actual time.

5.5. PROBLEMS WITH THE FILE FORMAT:

Though the file formats have been clearly instructed in the pamphlets, I received some of the files which have not followed the standardization which have been instructed by us. The margins, font type, font size, line space, etc., have been violated in some of the papers and they have to be carried out by me. The same file may be returned to the author to carry out the corrections.

The problems, which I have faced, are all not explored above as something is meant for discussion and something else meant for privacy. Don't think that I have hidden the details which are related with the data organization. The steps, which have been opted by me to organize the data, are fully discussed in this book. The pains and comments which I have received only have been hidden from your eyes as already I said that *something is meant for privacy and not for discussion*. Trust yourself only.

6

Recap

Some of the important things have been recapped here for the benefit of persons who are keen to organize seminars/conferences and are behind the designing of the database.

6.1. FOR ORGANIZERS

1. Make your choice whether you prefer the IT skilled professionals from outside or within your boundaries to carry out the system works.
2. Brief your expectations to the database organizer about what you do actually need from the database.
3. Let the database designer move with his/her works with work freedom so that they can do better.
4. It is advisable not to assign any other jobs which are not related to the database designers' desk as the other assignments may interrupt and keep them away from showing their performance in the works.
5. Offer sophisticated system and software infrastructure to carry out the tasks properly.

6. Don't force the database designers for any kind of output as they need little bit of time to satisfy your requirements. Chances are there to commit the mistakes in any part when they are hurried to finish the task by someone.

7. Don't let any other person who is not related with the database to work in it without the knowledge of the database designer under any circumstances. In Database and programming sector continuing others works always is a complex process as the designer of the Database/ programme only would be familiar with concepts which are adopted by them. If any others enter the works, they may be confused with the structure of the data organization and chances are there to collapse the entire database system which may require reorganizing the whole system from the beginning.

8. The works which are not related to the data organization should not be assigned to the designer even if the works are related with the seminars/ conferences. For instance the database organizer should not be called to carry out the routines which have been assigned to the food committee people as the local variations will definitely violate the data organization and leads to the poor performance. The designer should be in front of the system always so that the delegates who have come to attend the event can get enough details that may be related to the following.

    a. To verify the registration;

    b. To verify the DD/Cheque/Credit Card details, if any;

    c. To verify the author's name and other details;

d. To verify the Co-Authors' names and other details;

e. To verify accommodation related details. (Though a separate committee is there, database organizer has the required data about the accommodation committee details and hence enough details can be provided to the delegates when they are in need.)

f. To verify the address details;

g. To verify the phone/mobile details;

h. To verify the e-mail id details;

i. To verify the designation details;

j. To verify the institution details where they are in service.

9. Though we have enough printed outputs on our desk, the system access will make our works easier. So, the database designer should be near the registration section so as the delegates' doubts may be cleared.

10. The above things could be done by the database designer and his/her team only. Hence other kinds of works may be not assigned to them.

6.2. FOR DATABASE DESIGNERS

Abraham Silberschatz (et al) has brought out some of the global routine maintenance activities for the Database Administrators. They are;

i. Periodically backing up the database, either onto tapes or onto remote servers, to prevent loss of data in case of disasters such as flooding.

ii. Ensuring that enough free disk space is available for normal operation and upgrading disk space as required.

iii. Monitoring jobs running on the database and ensuring that performance is not degraded by very expensive tasks submitted by some users.

Apart from the above standard routines a few items that are concerned with the events have been categorized here.

1. Analyze yourself before accepting the job that whether you have the enough capacity to organize the data towards the database tools or not.
2. You must capture enough details on the routines, which are behind the seminars/conferences.
3. You should be ready to work hard always without having any restriction in your routines as you may need to work more time apart from your regular schedules, even if the day is a holiday.
4. Be sure about your authorities regarding the work freedom as it plays the major role to carry out your tasks. You must have freedom in your works. If you are sure that you will get the work freedom, then go on. Otherwise think twice before taking up the task, as you are the person who is going to take the whole responsibility of the data organization and hence credit or loss that will come to your desk.
5. Unless you take care of your routines, you are not supposed to expect or face the loss that means your performance will get suffered.
6. Permit a few persons who could be trusted by you to incorporate them into your works, which are related with the data verification jobs. Better choose the helper with required skills.
7. For entering the fee and some other information into the database there may be a need to have a person

with us so as the works could be easier. Remember that the person who is with you should not be replaced by someone else as flow of work continuity might suffer. The understanding between you and the helper is a must here and he/she must obey your commands is an important aspect. Non-cooperation and misunderstanding would always violate the works as well as performance also.

8. Kindly request the authorities that not to assign any other works to you when you are busy in data organization. As your desk is already loaded with some major tasks, it is not possible to do other works under someone who is responsible for the job that may bring misunderstandings between them and you, as they are not bothered about your work loads. Having the contrary opinions are quite natural among the human beings. Wherever you go and whatever the jobs you do, remember that differences are always there as the human nature differs from person to person. Someone may be polite and someone may be harsh. You can never expect all the people who are surrounding you to behave in a polite manner. Flexibility and tolerance are some of the essential things for the people who would like to get success in their target. Whether you like it or not, something requires compromise without which moving into our way is supposed to be not an easy job. It is universal truth that a person can never serve two masters and the same information can be captured from any of the reference sources, which are related with the principles of management. When this concept is violated, the performance of the works also would suffer. Remember that your desk may receive many unwanted comments and criticizing words from any direction that may disturb you to keep your concentration in the works. Concentrate on the real

time routines which make you to get success in your work.

9. If you need you may have consultation with any of the IT skilled person, who is close to you in order to structure a good database, as it requires a strong base to architect information.

10. Whatever the job you do, remember that there must be a chance to hear the positive comments which stimulate your works whereas the negative words might be ignored, as these comments may divert your mind set from the work which is on your desk, and also cause stress which might spoil your health also because these things are expected to be done by someone else who is always against you and your routine. Hence, ignore them and keep your mind on the right track.

7

Conclusion

My eyes raise while organizing the entire data of the event towards the application package WinISIS® as the powers of the said application are rigorous which enabled me to take up my works in an easy way to reach the target. Everything is possible when we have the entire technological infrastructure with adequately skilled professionals. As a database organizer we should not spell the word 'No', 'Never', 'Not Possible' that may degrade ones dignity and would also show that the level of confidence you have on yourself. Once when the tasks have been taken by us, they should be accomplished successfully; otherwise think twice before accepting any kind of task. Whatever output be required by the authorities, it might be generated within the stipulated time. Because the major tasks which are accepted by us would get more focus from all directions, as we are organizing the major event. So there may be a chance to face positive as well as negative comments, which stand in front of our desk that could be faced properly when we are sure about our works as well as our potentials. Sometimes this kind of experience would bring unnecessary stress to us that should not be allowed under any circumstances that could be possible by the way of approaching the problems which may differ from person to person. Feel free and don't get tempted which could be one of the reasons behind stress that would make your mind suffer as well as affect your works also. Remember that within the limited time we would have to finish our tasks, which should not be violated by any other factors. Your target should not be hid from your vision by these kinds of interruptions. Sharpen your vision to aim your target by the way of removing the interruptions which you have in front of your desk.

The method acquired by us to organize the data for any event may or may not be criticized by others. Remember that whatever be the way chosen by us would enable us to make the event success to make the authorities get satisfied with the routines. They would be satisfied when the required exact output could be generated from our desk only. Here we need not bother about others words which discourage the way of our works. Here I want to recall one thing for your information that "The ways may differ from person to person; but the target is the same." You need a tasty food that could be done by the chef. It is the responsibility of the chef to make the food as good as per our expectations. But we need not worry about the way of cooking, which is adopted by the chef. Like that the database organizer should have work freedom and it would not get any disturbance/ criticism from others. So keep it in your mind that as these kinds of interruptions would suffer our works, handle them with care to avoid unwanted things.

Experts say that there would be always some things in front of us. They are;

Good and evil. Right and Wrong.

We have to make our choice. As a teaching professionals we are here to select the good and right, not for bad and wrong as we should be a dedicated person to our profession.

Feel free and love your family, relatives, friends and everyone in the world that makes you happy and to acquire more confidence, involvement etc., in your work always.

Die for something is always better than Live for Nothing.

Good luck.

I humbly request the readers of this book to spend a few minutes of their valuable time to go through the next few pages, if they are really aware of Global Warming effects *as it is the responsibility of every one of the human beings who are living in this planet in order to secure the present generation as well as feature too*. The Top 50 things To Do To Stop Global Warming have been listed here. T*he original site from which this list was taken has been given below:*

http://globalwarming-facts.info You can find more at: *http://globalwarming-facts.info/2*

Global Warming is a dramatically urgent and serious problem. We don't need to wait for governments to find a solution for this problem: each individual can bring an important help adopting a more responsible lifestyle: starting from little, everyday things. It's the only reasonable way to save our planet, before it is too late. Here is a list of 50 simple things that everyone can do in order to fight against and reduce the Global Warming phenomenon: some of these ideas are at no cost, some other require a little effort or investment but can help you save a lot of money, in the middle long term!

1. Replace a regular incandescent light bulb with a compact fluorescent light bulb (cfls) CFLs use 60% less energy than a regular bulb. This simple switch will save about 300 pounds of carbon dioxide a year.
2. Install a programmable thermostat Programmable

thermostats will automatically lower the heat or air conditioning at night and raise them again in the morning. They can save you $100 a year on your energy bill.

3. Move your thermostat down 2° in winter and up 2° in summer Almost half of the energy we use in our homes goes to heating and cooling. You could save about 2,000 pounds of carbon dioxide a year with this simple adjustment.

4. Clean or replace filters on your furnace and air conditioner. Cleaning a dirty air filter can save 350 pounds of carbon dioxide a year.

5. Choose energy efficient appliances when making new purchases Look for the Energy Star label on new appliances to choose the most energy efficient products available.

6. Do not leave appliances on standby Use the "on/off" function on the machine itself. A TV set that's switched on for 3 hours a day (the average time Europeans spend watching TV) and in standby mode during the remaining 21 hours uses about 40% of its energy in standby mode.

7. Wrap your water heater in an insulation blanket You'll save 1,000 pounds of carbon dioxide a year with this simple action. You can save another 550 pounds per year by setting the thermostat no higher than 50°C.

8. Move your fridge and freezer Placing them next to the cooker or boiler consumes much more energy than if they were standing on their own. For example, if you put them in a hot cellar room where the room temperature is 30-35°C, energy use is almost double and causes an extra 160kg of CO2 emissions for fridges per year and 320kg for freezers.

9. Defrost old fridges and freezers regularly Even better is to replace them with newer models, which all have automatic defrost cycles and are generally up to two times more energy-efficient than their predecessors.

10. Don't let heat escape from your house over a long period When airing your house, open the windows for only a few minutes. If you leave a small opening all day long, the energy needed to keep it warm inside during six cold months (10°C or less outside temperature) would result in almost 1 ton of CO2 emissions.

11. Replace your old single-glazed windows with double-glazing This requires a bit of upfront investment, but will halve the energy lost through windows and pay off in the long term. If you go for the best the market has to offer (wooden-framed double-glazed units with low-emission glass and filled with argon gas), you can even save more than 70% of the energy lost.

12. Get a home energy audit Many utilities offer free home energy audits to find where your home is poorly insulated or energy inefficient. You can save up to 30% off your energy bill and 1,000 pounds of carbon dioxide a year. Energy Star can help you find an energy specialist.

13. Cover your pots while cooking doing so can save a lot of the energy needed for preparing the dish. Even better are pressure cookers and steamers: they can save around 70%!

14. Use the washing machine or dishwasher only when they are full If you need to use it when it is half full, then use the half-load or economy setting. There is also no need to set the temperatures high. Nowadays detergents are so efficient that they get your clothes and dishes clean at low temperatures.

15. Take a shower instead of a bath A shower takes up to four times less energy than a bath. To maximise the energy saving, avoid power showers and use low-flow showerheads, which are cheap and provide the same comfort.

16. Use less hot water It takes a lot of energy to heat water. You can use less hot water by installing a low flow showerhead (350 pounds of carbon dioxide saved per year) and washing your clothes in cold or warm water (500 pounds saved per year) instead of hot.

17. Use a clothesline instead of a dryer whenever possible You can save 700 pounds of carbon dioxide when you air dry your clothes for 6 months out of the year.

18. Insulate and weatherize your home Properly insulating your walls and ceilings can save 25% of your home heating bill and 2,000 pounds of carbon dioxide a year. Caulking and weather-stripping can save another 1,700 pounds per year. Energy Efficient has more information on how to better insulate your home.

19. Be sure you're recycling at home. You can save 2,400 pounds of carbon dioxide a year by recycling half of the waste your household generates.

20. Recycle your organic waste Around 3% of the greenhouse gas emissions through the methane is released by decomposing bio-degradable waste. By recycling organic waste or composting it if you have a garden, you can help eliminate this problem! Just make sure that you compost it properly, so it decomposes with sufficient oxygen, otherwise your compost will cause methane emissions and smell foul.

21. Buy intelligently One bottle of 1.5l requires less energy and produces less waste than three bottles of 0.5l. As well, buy recycled paper products: it takes less 70 to

90% less energy to make recycled paper and it prevents the loss of forests worldwide.

22. Choose products that come with little packaging and buy refills when you can You will also cut down on waste production and energy use... another help against global warming.

23. Reuse your shopping bag When shopping, it saves energy and waste to use a reusable bag instead of accepting a disposable one in each shop. Waste not only discharges CO2 and methane into the atmosphere, it can also pollute the air, groundwater and soil.

24. Reduce waste Most products we buy cause greenhouse gas emissions in one or another way, e.g. during production and distribution. By taking your lunch in a reusable lunch box instead of a disposable one, you save the energy needed to produce new lunch boxes.

25. Plant a tree A single tree will absorb one ton of carbon dioxide over its lifetime. Shade provided by trees can also reduce your air conditioning bill by 10 to 15%. The Arbor Day Foundation has information on planting and provides trees you can plant with membership.

26. Switch to green power In many areas, you can switch to energy generated by clean, renewable sources such as wind and solar. In some of these, you can even get refunds by government if you choose to switch to a clean energy producer, and you can also earn money by selling the energy you produce and don't use for yourself.

27. Buy locally grown and produced foods The average meal in the United States travels 1,200 miles from the farm to your plate. Buying locally will save fuel and keep money in your community.

28. Buy fresh foods instead of frozen Frozen food uses 10 times more energy to produce.
29. Seek out and support local farmers markets They reduce the amount of energy required to grow and transport the food to you by one fifth. Seek farmer's markets in your area, and go for them.
30. Buy organic foods as much as possible Organic soils capture and store carbon dioxide at much higher levels than soils from conventional farms. If we grew all of our corn and soybeans organically, we'd remove 580 billion pounds of carbon dioxide from the atmosphere!
31. Eat less meat Methane is the second most significant greenhouse gas and cows are one of the greatest methane emitters. Their grassy diet and multiple stomachs cause them to produce methane, which they exhale with every breath.
32. Reduce the number of miles you drive by walking, biking, carpooling or taking mass transit wherever possible Avoiding just 10 miles of driving every week would eliminate about 500 pounds of carbon dioxide emissions a year! Look for transit options in your area.
33. Start a carpool with your coworkers or classmates Sharing a ride with someone just 2 days a week will reduce your carbon dioxide emissions by 1,590 pounds a year. eRideShare.com runs a free service connecting north american commuters and travelers.
34. Don't leave an empty roof rack on your car This can increase fuel consumption and CO2 emissions by up to 10% due to wind resistance and the extra weight - removing it is a better idea.
35. Keep your car tuned up Regular maintenance helps improve fuel efficiency and reduces emissions. When

just 1% of car owners properly maintain their cars, nearly a billion pounds of carbon dioxide are kept out of the atmosphere.

36. Drive carefully and do not waste fuel You can reduce CO2 emissions by readjusting your driving style. Choose proper gears, do not abuse the gas pedal, use the engine brake instead of the pedal brake when possible and turn off your engine when your vehicle is motionless for more than one minute. By readjusting your driving style you can save money on both fuel and car mantainance.

37. Check your tires weekly to make sure they're properly inflated Proper tire inflation can improve gas mileage by more than 3%. Since every gallon of gasoline saved keeps 20 pounds of carbon dioxide out of the atmosphere, every increase in fuel efficiency makes a difference!

38. When it is time for a new car, choose a more fuel efficient vehicle You can save 3,000 pounds of carbon dioxide every year if your new car gets only 3 miles per gallon more than your current one. You can get up to 60 miles per gallon with a hybrid! You can find information on fuel efficiency on FuelEconomy and on GreenCars websites.

39. Try car sharing Need a car but don't want to buy one? Community car sharing organizations provide access to a car and your membership fee covers gas, maintenance and insurance. Many companies - such as Flexcar - offer low emission or hybrid cars too! Also, see ZipCar.

40. Try telecommuting from home Telecommuting can help you drastically reduce the number of miles you drive every week. For more information, check out the

Telework Coalition.

41. **Fly less :** Air travel produces large amounts of emissions so reducing how much you fly by even one or two trips a year can reduce your emissions significantly. You can also offset your air travel carbon emissions by investingin renewable energy projects.

42. **Encourage your school or business to reduce emissions:** You can extend your positive influence on global warming well beyond your home by actively encouraging other to take action.

43. **Join the virtual march :** The Stop Global Warming Virtual March is a non-political effort to bring people concerned about global warming together in one place. Add your voice to the hundreds of thousands of other people urging action on this issue.

44. **Encourage the switch to renewable energy :** Successfully combating global warming requires a national transition to renewable energy sources such as solar, wind and biomass. These technologies are ready to be deployed more widely but there are regulatory barriers impeding them. U.S. citizens, take action to break down those barriers with Vote Solar.

45. **Protect and conserve forest worldwide :** Forests play a critial role in global warming: they store carbon. When forests are burned or cut down, their stored carbon is release into the atmosphere - deforestation now accounts for about 20% of carbon dioxide emissions each year. Conservation International has more information on saving forests from global warming.

46. **Consider the impact of your investments :** If you invest your money, you should consider the impact that your investments and savings will have on global

warming. Check out Social Invest and Ceres to can learn more about how to ensure your money is being invested in companies, products and projects that address issues related to climate change.

47. **Make your city cool :** Cities and states around the country have taken action to stop global warming by passing innovative transportation and energy saving legislation. If you're in the U.S., join the cool cities list.

48. **Tell Congress to act :** The McCain Lieberman Climate Stewardship and Innovation Act would set a firm limit on carbon dioxide emissions and then use free market incentives to lower costs, promote efficiency and spur innovation. Tell your representative to support it.

49. **Make sure your voice is heard! :** Americans must have a stronger commitment from their government in order to stop global warming and implement solutions and such a commitment won't come without a dramatic increase in citizen lobbying for new laws with teeth. Get the facts about U.S. politicians and candidates at Project Vote Smart and The League of Conservation Voters. Make sure your voice is heard by voting!

50. **Share this list! :** Send this page via e-mail to your friends! Spread this list worldwide and help people doing their part: the more people you will manage to enlighten, the greater YOUR help to save the planet will be (but please take action on first person too)!

Thanks for spending your valuable time and remember that you are not going to save others only. You and your family members also are in the same boundaries. Please try to be the first person to implement the said items and contribute your part to secure the planet.

Annexures

ANNEXURE-I

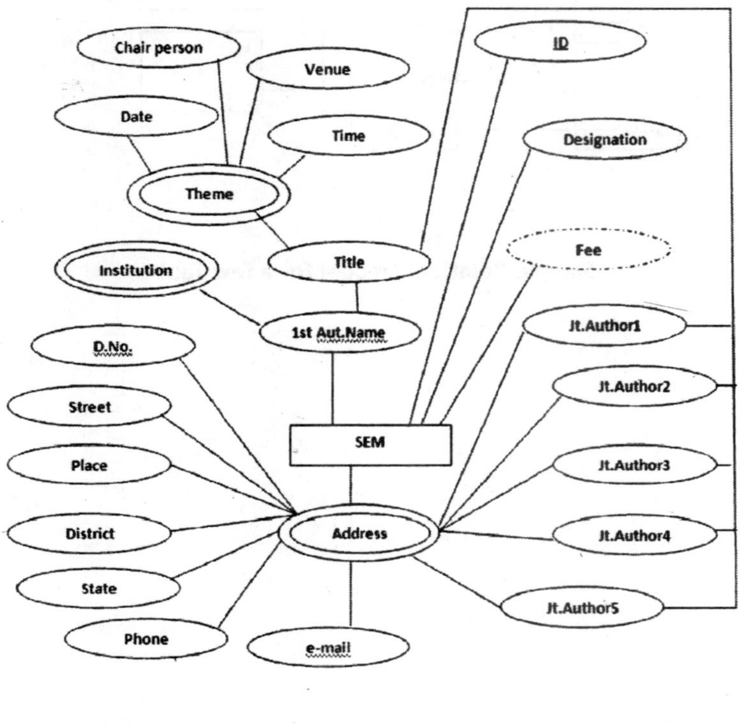

E-R diagram with single, composite and derived attributes

ANNEXURE-II

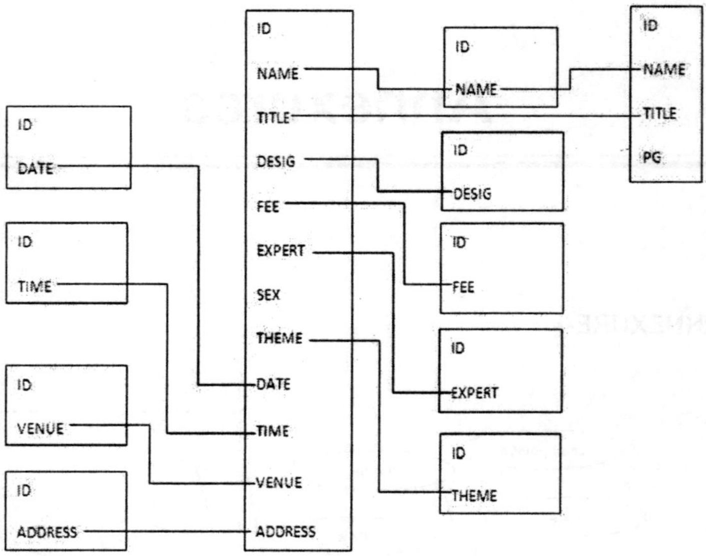

Sample Relational model for a few Tables

ANNEXURE-III

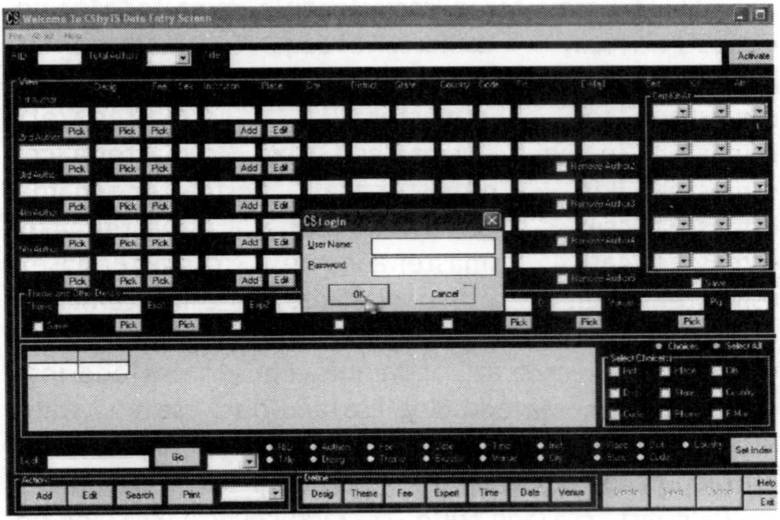

Data Entry Screen of CSbyTs

ANNEXURE-IV

Sample Query to execute authors' details:

SELECT csmaster.id, csmaster.title, csmaster.a1name, csmaster.a1sex, csmaster.a1cer, csmaster.a1kit, csmaster.a1att, csmaster.a2name, csmaster.a2sex, csmaster.a2cer, csmaster.a2kit csmaster.a2att, csmaster.a3name, csmaster.a3sex csmaster.a3cer, csmaster.a3kit, csmaster.a3att, csmaster.a4name, csmaster.a4sex, csmaster.a4cer, csmaster.a4kit, csmaster.a4att, csmaster.a5name, csmaster.a5sex, csmaster.a5cer, csmaster.a5kit, csmaster.a5att, cstheme.theme, csdesig.desig, csfee.fee, csexpert.expert, cstime.time, csdt.dt, csvenue.venue, csa1add.inst, csa1add.place, csa1add.city, csa1add.dist, csa1add.state, csa1add.country, csa1add.ph, csa1add.mail, csa1add.pcode, csa2add.inst, csa2add.place, csa2add.city, csa2add.dist, csa2add.state, csa2add.country, csa2add.ph, csa2add.mail, csa2add.pcode, csa3add.inst, csa3add.place, csa3add.city, csa3add.dist, csa3add.state, csa3add.country, csa3add.ph, csa3add.mail, csa3add.pcode, csa4add.inst, csa4add.place, csa4add.city, csa4add.dist, csa4add.state, csa4add.country, csa4add.ph, csa4add.mail, csa4add.pcode, csa5add.inst, csa5add.place, csa5add.city, csa5add.dist, csa5add.state, csa5add.country, csa5add.ph, csa5add.mail, csa5add.pcode FROM csmaster, csdesig, csfee, csa1add, csa2add, csa3add, csa4add, csa5add, csexpert, cstheme, cstime, csdt, csvenue WHERE (((csmaster.a1desig)<>False) AND ((csmaster.a2desig)<>False) AND ((csmaster.a3desig)<>False) AND ((csmaster.a4desig)<>False) AND ((csmaster.a5desig)=[csdesig].[id]) AND ((csmaster.a1fee)<>False) AND ((csmaster.a2fee)<>False) AND ((csmaster.a3fee)<>False) AND ((csmaster.a4fee) <>False) AND ((csmaster.a5fee)=[csfee].[id]) AND ((csmaster.a1add) =[csa1add].[id]) AND ((csmaster.a2add)

=[csa2add].[id]) AND ((csmaster.a3add)=[csa3add].[id]) AND ((csmaster.a4add) =[csa4add].[id]) AND ((csmaster.a5add)= [csa5add].[id]) AND ((csmaster.expert1)<>False) AND ((csmaster.expert2) <>False) AND ((csmaster.expert3)= [csexpert].[id]) AND ((csmaster.theme)=[cstheme].[id]) AND ((csmaster.time)=[cstime].[id]) AND ((csmaster.dt)= [csdt].[id]) AND *((csmaster.venue)=[csvenue].[id])) order by csmaster.id;*

Bibliography

Abraham Silherschatz, Henry F.Korth and Sudarshan, S. *Database System Concepts*. New Delhi. MGGraw-Hill.2002.

Akotia, P. *Financial Records Management Project: Phase Three*. Kampala: Department for International development.2004.

Andrew Buxton and Alan Hopkinson. *The CDS/ISIS for Windows Handbook*. Paris. Unesco/CI.2001

Aziz, S et.al. "A Simulation of an Event Building Network for the CMS High Energy Physics Experiment" *SCI 2003 7th World Multiconference on Systemics, Cybernatics and Informatics*. 27-30. July. 2003.

Cain, P and Millar, L. "Authenticity of electronic records: a report prepared for UNESCO and International Council of Archives." London:ICA.2004.

Cox, R. "Electronic Records Management: re-defining electronic records management." *Records Management Quarterly.* 1996.

George Koch and Kevin Loney. *Oracle 8: The Complete Reference*, New Delhi.Tata McGraw-Hill.1999.

International Council on Archives. "Guide for managing e-records." *http://www.interactions.org/alpi/enews_NEPAD.html (accessed 05 sep 2010).*

International Records Management Trust. *The E-Records Readiness Tool*. London.IRMT.2004.

Keakopa, S.M. "Automated records management systems in the ESARBICA region." *ESARBICA*. 21(1).41-9.2002.

Knowledge Management Glossary. "Knowledge Management." *http:// www.k-solutions.com/ members/avanti/avanti2020.nsflallpages/ knowledge%20management%20Glossary* (accessed 16 Oct 2010)

Lancaster, F.W. and Climenson, W.D."Evaluating the Economic Efficiency of a Document Retrieval System." *J.Docum*. 24(1).16-40.1968.

Menne-Haritz, A. "Dynamic knowledge in organizational environments" Workshop on distributed cognition and distributed knowledge: Key issues in design for E-Commerce and E-Government.14-15.June 2000.*http:/ /falcon.ifs.unilinz. ac.at/workshop/ index.html*(accessed 12 Aug 2010)

Michael Abbey and Michael J. Corey. *ORACLE: A Beginners Guide*, Newdelhi,Tata McGraw-Hill, 34.1997.

Mnjama, N. and Wamukoya, J. "E-government and e-records management." Paper presented at the SADC Workshop on E-government, Gaborone, 14-16 April.2004.

Nicholas, D. and Rowlands, I. *The Internet: Its Impact and Evaluation*. London. Aslib.2000.

Nonaka, I. and Takeuchi, H. *The knowledge creating company*. London. Oxford University Press.1995.

O'Brien, A.J. *Management Information Systems: A Managerial End User Perspective*.2nd ed. Burr Ridge, IL. Irwin.1993.

Orna, E. *Information Strategy in Practice*. Aldershot: Gover,

P.7.2004.

Pollis, A R. "Local choice and Local Commitment: Respons". *Information Technology.* Ed. Allen kent and Thomas J. Galvin. New York. Marcel dekker,inc.1982.

Reed, B. "Electronic records management in Australia." *Records management journal.*7(3).1-13.1997.

Roper, M and Millar, L.(eds). *Managing Electronic Records.* London.IRMT.1999.

Rosenfeld, L and Morville, P. *Information Architecture for the World Wide Web.* Sebastopol, CA: O'Reilly,p.4.2002.

Saravanan T."WINISIS: A Birds eye view."*IJILS.* Vol.19.N1-2.Jan-June.2006.

Saravanan T."Harnessing Database for Indian Journal of Information, Library & Society(IJILIS) using WINISIS: An Attempt." Vol-20. N 3-4. Dec 2007.

Saravanan T."A Visualization Interface Supporting Bibliographic Retrieval in Higher Educational Sector."*DLIBCOM.* Vol.-3. Issue-1.January 2008.

Saravanan T."TS: An Emerging Visualized Interface for Files Organization." *Humanities.*Vol-45.Annamalai University.2008.

Saravanan T."A LIS Dissertation Abstracts Database: An Experience with WINISIS."*Information Studies.*Vol-14.No.3.July 2008.

Saravanan T. "Emerging Self learning Graphical Interface in LIS Discipline :A Glance." Library Progress.Vol.29. No.1. 2009.

Saravanan T."WWW: How does it should be?." *UGC Sponsored National Seminar.* DLIS, Annamalai University. 27-27 March 2009.

Saravanan T. "Use of Winisis for Compiling Abstract of dissertations submitted by all faculties of Annamalai University Tamilnadu: An Attempt." *SRELS*. Vol.47. No.1.Feb 2010.

Simens, G. "Content Management: Our organized future." *http:/ /www. elearnspace.org/Articles/content management.htm*(accessed 10 october 2010)

Software Perfect. "Content Management Software." *http:/ /www. softwareperfect.com/cms_software/content management _system .htm* (acessed 10 october 2010)

Srimurugan, A. "Ranganathan Speeks...A Dialogue with Dr.S.Ranganathan in the Presence of Prof. M.R.Kumbar : A Simulation." *Seminar on Strategic Information Management in the Digital Era*. 26 & 27 Mar. 61-62. 2009

Stephen M. Mutula and Justus m. Wamukoya. "Web information management." Great Britain. Chandos.2007.

Trippe, B. and Walter, M. *Content management and Web Publishing: The Columbia Guide to Digital Publishing. New York. Columbia University Press.2003.*

Vickery, B.C. *On Retrieval System Theory.2nd ed.* London, Butterworths.1965.

White, M."Content management systems for intranets." P.46-50.2005.

Wig, K.M. "Supporting Knowledge management: A selection of methods and techniques."*Expert Systems with Applications*. 13(1).15-27.1997.

Wikipedia. "Content management system." *http:/ /www. Enwikipedia.org/wiki/ content_management_ system*(accessed 10 october 2010)

Zbigniew M. Nowicki. *New features of the WinISIS system, Geneva.2001.*

http://iainstitute.org/pg/about_us.php(accessed (accessed 17 Aug 2010)

*http://www.motive.co.nz/glossary/information.php(*accessed 17 Aug 2010)

http://www.businessdictionary.com/definition/information-architecture.html (accessed 19 sep 2010)

http://globalwarming-facts.info (accessed 10 Feb 2011)

Index

S

T

U

V

W